LEAVE YOUR BIG BEHAVIOR IN YOUR HOME CORRAL

LIBELOUS RHYMES AND SCANDALOUS EXAMPLES

OF Historical Distortions AND Southwestern Apocrypha

By Michael Coyote Peach

Published by Sedona Heritage Publishing, held by the Sedona Historical Society, Inc.

Visit Our Website

www.sedonamuseum.org

Like us on Facebook

Facebook.com/sedonamuseum

View Our Calendar of Events

Sedonamuseum.org/calendar

Printed in the United States of America

Acknowledgements

I must begin here by thanking the great people at the Sedona Historical Society whose Publication Committee made this book possible. Bill Levengood, Publication Chairman, extended the original invitation that led to my first book, <u>The Facts Keep Gettin' in the Way of the Story</u>, and let it be known that the next one could go to press as soon as I had it ready. As he did for "The Facts…," Bill formatted the text and oversaw any editorial changes. Unlike some of the material in my first book, almost all of the poems in this book were written specifically as performance pieces for my shows at the Sedona Heritage Museum and other venues. Performing this material before live audiences gives me the ability to shape it more in accordance with the oral traditions which gave birth to this type of storytelling. Consequently the texts of some of these poems contain lines or verses which I do not include when performing them live. Invaluable assistance in presenting these performances is provided by the wonderful – and mostly volunteer – staff at the Sedona Heritage Museum, including Janeen Trevillyan, Kathie Hamblin, Ray Anderson, Dave Thomas, Ron Maasen, Cynthia Batchelder, Bill Etter, Loretta Benore, Ann Pearson, Ruth Clem, Valerie Girard, Jane Petty, Morna Paule, Joan Miller, Mary Clement, Fran Levengood, Terry Greene, Janet Sage, Carol Thomas, Lou Anne Scott, Lisa Hyatt, Pam Dorris, Karen Gossler, Barbara Shambach, Brad Elliot, Pat Dimillo, and Nicole Dean.

I continue to be indebted to the researches and scholarship of many established southwestern historians, authors, editors and aficionados. Among this number are Arizona State Historian Marshall Trimble, <u>True West Magazine</u> and True West blog publisher Bob Boze Bell, Roscoe G. Willson, Patricia Limerick, C.L. Sonnichen, Leo W. Banks, Charles D. Lauer, Ben Traywick, John Myers, Craig Childs, Herbert V. Young, John Boesseneker, Mark Boardman, Douglas D. Martin, William Howard, Bill Roberts, Robert Mason, Dorothy D. Anderson and Richard Kimball. I have noted individual sources of inspiration and information in the introductions to the various poems.

Some compilation works deserve particular mention, <u>Those Early Days, Old Timers' Memoirs of Oak Creek, Sedona, and the Verde Valley Region of Northern Arizona</u>, compiled by the Sedona Westerners and republished by the Sedona Historical Society; <u>Pioneer Stories of Arizona's Verde Valley</u>, compiled and published by the Verde Valley Pioneers Association; and <u>Echoes of the Past, Tales of Old Yavapai in Arizona</u>, compiled and published by the Yavapai Cow Belles of Arizona. These volumes are invaluable sources of firsthand accounts of the early history of central Arizona. National Public Radio and wikipedia.org also get a nod here for providing occasional tidbits and sources for further research.

My very patient and loving wife Jane continues to be a source of support and honest criticism as both a sounding board and reader, and also as a technical guide whenever my Luddite tendencies befuddle me.

The title of this book is a phrase from a true story, The Murder Steer, by Bret McGuire.

All of the images were sourced from public domain sites, but I want to thank Karen, a.k.a. the Graphics Fairy at thegraphicsfairy.com for the elephant, a couple of chickens, and the dragons.

The author photo was taken by Sedona Historical Society President Dave Thomas. Front and rear cover photos are by the author.

Introduction

Mike Peach is a great friend and contributor to the Sedona Heritage Museum. We are proud to once again help to bring one of his books into publication. This is Mike's second book. Mike's mastery of poetry is only exceeded by the amount of research that goes into each of his books. As you will see in the following pages, Mike searches far and wide to find just the right "off the wall" stories that will delight the mind and enlighten the soul. Mike's great sense of humor, extensive vocabulary, and vast knowledge of western folk lore give him the ability to tell a great story.

Mike puts history in a whole new light. You may know that Arizona became a state in 1912 or that the shootout at the OK Corral happened in Tombstone, but what do you know of the "Gunfight at Big Hat"? You know of P.T. Barnum but what about Lloyd Olsen and "Miracle Mike the Headless Wonder Chicken"?

Everyone has heard of Wyatt Earp, but what do you know of Andrew Doran and the "Graham County Train Robbery"? Zane Grey was noted as a great author of western tales, but Gladwell Richardson wrote over 300 stories (under some 29 pen names).

And when it comes to fashion, we think of Lauren, Dior, Calvin Klein, Versace and many others, but wait till you read how E.L. Bradshaw redesigned a brand new shirt in "Hasta La Vista, Fashionista". Don't miss Aida Ferrara's new use for stockings in "The Lady with the Lethal Lingerie".

All of Mike's poems have deeper meaning between the lines or sometimes just in the title, as in "Some Days the Bear Eats You".

In all, as you read this book, you will laugh, maybe cry, you'll learn some history you didn't know. You'll ponder the different points of view and you'll enjoy.

Bill Levengood
Sedona Heritage Publishing

"None of us can escape history…
    We will be remembered in spite of ourselves."
                                    Abraham Lincoln

"History is a cruel joke played on the dead by the living."
                                    Anonymous

For Bill, Gloria, Pat & Pamme
with love

Author's Preface

They Had No Poet and So They Died

In the dim waste land of the Orient stands
The wreck of a race so old and vast
That the grayest legend cannot lay hands
On a single fact of its tongueless past.
Nor even the red gold crown of a king
Nor a warrior's shield nor aught beside,
Can history out of the ruins ring –
They had no poet – and so they died.

Babel and Nineveh, what are they
But feeble hints of a passing power
That over the populous East held sway
In a dream of pomp for a paltry hour.
A toppled tower and a shattered stone
Where the satyrs dance and the dragons hide,
Is all that is known of the glory flown –
They had no poet and so they died.

Down where the dolorous Congo slips
Like a tawny snake through the torrid clime,
Man's soul has slept in a cold eclipse,
On the world's dark rim since the dawn of time.
And if ever the ancient Nubians wrought
A work of beauty, or strength, or pride,
It was unrecorded, and goes for naught –
They had no poet and so they died.

In the lonely southwest, by the tropic seas,
In the land of summer, and sun, and gold,
'Tis said that a nation as grand as Greece,
Up grew in the glorious days of old;
But Time, the leveler, came at last,
And scattered its splendors far and wide,
And the marvelous Aztec empire passed –
They had no poet and so they died.

And even here in the sun-crowned West,
In the land we love, in the vales we've trod,
Where the bleeding palms of the world find rest,
On Freedom's lap at the feet of God –
Even here, I say, ere the earth waxed old,
A race Titanic did once abide,
But ah! Their story is left untold –
They had no poet and so they died.

The lines above were printed in the *Tombstone Epitaph* and credited to "Exchange" which was a term signifying a common source from which various news and literary items could be extracted for use by newsmen in need of filler material, much as wire services supply our modern newspapers.

The poem's author was Dr. James Newton Matthews (1852-1910) who was called "The Prairie Poet" and was, at the age of sixteen, the first student to enroll at the University of Illinois at Urbana-Champaign when it opened in 1868. The poem was printed in Volume VI, issue Number 154 of *The Current*, a weekly news magazine published in Chicago on November 27, 1886.

It is easy to see what probably attracted the *Epitaph's* editor to this poem. The West is mentioned specifically ("at the feet of God" no less!), and contemporary citizens of Tombstone might read these words and wonder if, had the Aztecs only been saved by poetry and the higher arts, Montezuma's progeny might not have degenerated into the scurrilous marauding Apaches. In spite of my sarcastic tone here, I enjoy this poem. But Matthew's verse reveals him to be a man of his time. His reference to the "marvelous Aztec empire passing unrecorded" reflects the nation-centric self-assurance of American Manifest Destiny. The Spanish had trampled the Aztecs and, burning all but a handful of codices, had branded them as man-eating savages, incapable of the humanity required for lofty verse. And America had bested first the Spaniards and then the Mexicans, wresting Texas, California, and ultimately half of their North American holdings from them and thereby seizing the mantle of western hemispheric dominance. Surely this was proof of our inherent national superiority.

Matthew lived in a time in which these recently-acquired wild lands were being tamed. History was being made, and because the American mind grasped the importance of higher culture, future generations would know our glories and our achievements. And from this ivory tower of American exceptionalism, Matthew cast his enlightened gaze back through time and, while lamenting the presumed lack of literature, scholarship, and poetry among the Orientals, Babylonians, Nubians, and other "lesser" peoples, acquiesced to the contemporary view of their historical unworthiness. And yet the Spanish conquest had introduced an alphabet with which the ancient Nahuatl (Aztec) language was translated into literature, and beautiful poetry from its oral traditions was printed in the sixteenth century.

The deciphering of ancient Egyptian hieroglyphs made serious progress as of 1822, and Persian cuneiform texts were considered deciphered by 1857. This of course doesn't even take into account what might have been known had the great library at Alexandria, Egypt not been repeatedly burned between 48 BC to AD 642 by the Romans, Coptics, and Muslims; and that of the sixty-odd surviving classical Greek plays, the majority are attributed to four playwrights who were not the most frequent winners of the competitions for which these works were created. But in the zeitgeist of Matthew's latter nineteenth century intellectualism, these things were of little consequence. The garbled utterances of earlier cultures, despite their pretenses to grandeur, fell short of Shakespearean standards. Theirs was not *poetry*. And even while viewing them through a prism of cultural chauvinism, he seems here to almost pity them.

But Matthew's inspiration for this poem dates from a time when such linguistic and literary breakthroughs had not yet taken place. He seems almost certainly to have received his impetus from an Ode written by Alexander Pope:

"Vain was the chief's, the sage's pride! They had no poet, and they died.
In vain they schemed, in vain they bled! They had no poet, and are dead."

From Odes, Book 4, Ode 9, reported by William Warburton (1751).

And this combination of Pope and Matthews seems to have inspired the following in which the poet acknowledges at least one of his muses:

> *"Vain was the chief's, the sage's pride!*
> *They had no poet and they died."* -- **POPE.**

> BY Tigris, or the streams of Ind,
> Ere Colchis rose, or Babylon,
> Forgotten empires dreamed and sinned,
> Setting tall towns against the dawn,
> Which, when the proud Sun smote upon,
> Flashed fire for fire and pride for pride;
> Their names were . . . Ask oblivion! . . .
> *"They had no poet, and they died."*

> Queens, dusk of hair and tawny-skinned,
> That loll where fellow leopards fawn . . .
> Their hearts are dust before the wind,
> Their loves, that shook the world, are wan!
> Passion is mighty . . . but, anon,
> Strong Death has Romance for his bride;
> Their legends . . . Ask oblivion! . . .
> *"They had no poet, and they died."*

Heroes, the braggart trumps that dinned
    Their futile triumphs, monarch, pawn,
Wild tribesmen, kingdoms disciplined,
    Passed like a whirlwind and were gone;
They built with bronze and gold and brawn,
    The inner Vision still denied;
Their conquests . . . Ask oblivion! . . .
    "They had no poet, and they died."

Dumb oracles, and priests withdrawn,
    Was it but flesh they deified?
Their gods were . . . Ask oblivion! . . .
    "They had no poet, and they died."

Don Marquis
from <u>Dreams and Dust</u> (1915)

Donald Robert Perry Marquis (1878-1937) was a newspaper man, humorist, and poet best remembered for his stories about a cockroach named Archie and a cat named Mehitabel.

I wish I had discovered these two works prior to publishing my first book. They would have served nicely as an introduction to my poem, The Killing of Sedona Sue, which owes its aegis to Robert W. Service's The Shooting of Dan McGrew. But the main reason I've included them here is that ultimately Pope, Matthews, and Marquis are all saying the same thing – civilization's advance marches to the cadence of the troubadour. For all of the bombastic speeches, factual reportage, and interpretations (and *re*interpretations) of what is sanctioned as "the historical record", it is the artists and poets whose works convey the truest spirit of the age. As William Carlos Williams wrote in 1955: *It is difficult to get the news from poems, yet men die miserably every day for lack of what is found there.* And while I would not equate my scribblings to the caliber of the above-cited authors, I have in my own small way attempted here to shine light on some lesser-known characters and events. And while most of the poems contained herein are about actual people and events, and while satire is my objective, I mean no real disrespect to their reputations or to their memories (except in the case of professional politicians).

These poems are written in the popular tradition of the "Wild West" (factual or fictional), so if you are going to read them aloud, I suggest adopting a loud and twangy accent that befits bodacious yarn-spinning.

Table of Contents

"Captain" John Hance

"Captain" is in quotations because Hance did not earn an officer's rank during military service. It is conjectured that Grand Canyon visitors bestowed it on him as an honorary title reflecting his command of the canyon's history and geography. He is credited with having been the Grand Canyon's first permanent white resident, and on his death in 1919 (the year the canyon became a National Park) he was the first person buried in the Grand Canyon Pioneer Cemetery. Although he originally came to the canyon as a homesteader and prospector in 1880, he earned his principle livelihood and his lasting reputation as a guide and raconteur. The trail he created to reach his asbestos diggings became the first tourist trail into the canyon, known today as the New Hance Trail (a.k.a. the Red Canyon Trail). Hance Rapids on the Colorado River also bears his name. Together with William Hull he built a log hotel on the south rim near Grandview and established a stage coach route connecting it to Flagstaff. Having driven over that rutted route myself, I can imagine that no matter how Spartan the hotel's accommodations may have been, they would have been seen as a welcome deliverance from the tortures of an eighty-mile bone-jarring ride in a stagecoach!

Joseph Mulhatton and Gladwell Richardson – both are discussed in this volume – might have taken lessons on using the media to promote tourism from John Hance. Leo Banks and Craig Childs, in their book <u>Grand Canyon Stories Then and Now</u>, tell of how *The Coconino Weekly Sun* reported in May of 1892 that one of its reporters had accompanied Hance on a search for a "wild woman" rumored to be living in the canyon and that, together with the assistance of Hance's dog, they managed to capture the feral female and bring her to the canyon's rim. She was christened "Effie" and was reported to be drawing large numbers of tourists. The article conjectured that more of Effie's kind were believed to be dwelling in the canyon's depths and that plans were being made to bring them into civilization's embrace. "The cry is more wild girls or bust" reported the *Sun* on June 9th. (The paper's editor seems to have joined into the spirit of the gag.) Not many days later the paper ran an article stating that its coverage of this story had been greeted with skepticism by its readers, and no further mentions were made of Effie or of her alleged sister amazons.

Tourists were fair game for Hance's wit. Another anecdote reported by Banks and Childs tells of him cautioning a group of hikers about to descend to the canyon's bottom that the heat along the Colorado River had been known to melt the wings off of flies. A lady from New England is then said to have asked, "My goodness! How do the tourists stand it?" To which Hance replied, "Madam, I have never seen a tourist with wings."

Hance lost the tip of one of his fingers in a mining accident and when asked about it, he was known to claim that he'd "plumb worn it off pointing out all of this beautiful scenery." When asked by tourists how the canyon had come to be, he was fond of replying, "I dug it." In a Paul Bunyon-esque vein, he added that the dirt pile resulting from his excavations had become the San Francisco Peaks, outside of Flagstaff. Another of Hance's best-known tales is a variation on the one in my poem. In it, he tells of how sometimes fog would cover the canyon from rim to rim. Hance maintained that sometimes this fog was so thick that he could walk on it using snowshoes, or, upping the ante, that it would support both he and Darby – he named all of his horses and mules "Darby" so as to avoid forgetting which one he was talking about – allowing them to take a short cut directly across the canyon. On one such occasion, when they were only about half way across, the sun came out and began to disperse the fog! Valiant Darby leapt from patch to patch, but at length they fell through a hole and found themselves stranded atop Zoroaster Temple. A month passed before another fog blanketed the canyon. "It was a light fog," the Captain commented dryly. "But by then me and Darby was a whole lot lighter too."

Another Hance yarn tells of how a team of his prize mules were stolen by a gang of rough outlaws. He trailed them to their camp only to discover that they had butchered the animals and were just sitting down to a supper of mule stew! But the desperados had not counted on the incredible discipline Hance had instilled in those mules. Just as the thieves had all taken their first mouthfuls, he loudly called out, "Whoa, mule!" The obedient mule meat stuck in the outlaws' throats, stubbornly refusing to budge. As the helpless men lay gasping for breath, Hance walked into their camp and calmly disarmed them.

As this final, well-known Hance story shows, the Captain seems to have reveled in his reputation. He was regaling a group of tourists when someone in the crowd asked him if the hunting was any good there around the canyon.

"I'll say it is," said Hance. "Why, just this morning I bagged two five-point bucks!"

"That's very interesting," said the stranger. "Do you know who I am?"

Hance replied that he'd never seen the man before.

"Well," proclaimed the man, "I'm the Game Warden!"

"Well..." drawled the Captain, "do you know who I am? I'm the biggest damn liar in all of Arizona!"

"Captain" John Hance

"Captain" John Hance was a master of romance on a scale phantasmagorical.
By stretching the truth he'd grown long in the tooth,
And well known as a Grand Canyon Oracle.
A well-worn yarn he'd trot out of the barn on almost any occasion.
He'd exercise his choppers and pop out a whopper
At the slightest provocation.
When it came to banter, one of his standards he'd embellished with abandon,
Concerned the time that to save their lives, his horse had to jump the canyon!
This was a favorite, and he loved to relate it to gullible, tenderfoot tourists.
Such naive guests would seldom protest (unless they were factual purists).

"Them Injuns was mad and the odds were bad,
And our chances looked pretty slim.
Hemmed in on three sides, the only way to survive
Was to jump from the canyon's rim!
So I threw down my gun and ol' Darby took a run,
And he launched us out into the air.
Now that's miles across, but my ol' Darby hoss was a jumper beyond compare.
We was sailin' over clouds, and I was laughin' out loud
At the state of those Injuns' frustration,
When ol' Darby looked back and it threw him off track.
Musta busted his concentration.
The next thing I knowed, we was droppin' like a load
Of rocks toward the Colorado River!
The ground was a-comin' fast, and it looked like we'd be smashed,
But right about then I remembered –
I've always maintained that ol' Darby was trained to respond to my every demand.
So if I wanted to stop this precipitous drop, all I need do is give the command.
So I hollered out "Whoa!"
And we started to slow as ol' Darby he jammed his hooves down.
And we came to a halt well below Heaven's vault
Hangin' just a few feet off the ground."

And here the good captain would pause for reaction,
And to allow for a moment's introspection.

For, as you might have guessed, this narrative's success
Relied on an obvious question.
So here he might frown, or cast his gaze down,
But he usually didn't have too long to wait.
With his skill as a storyteller, some gal or some feller
By now would have swallowed the bait:
"Well, now, captain, you're here, so that makes it clear you survived –
And we're all glad of course!
Because a fall like that can be the death of a man…
But captain, what happened to your horse?"

And now Hance's task was to keep his face a mask,
And not yet to show them his grin.
Because much of the joy he derived from this ploy
Was to gradually reel his fish in.
"Well, let's see…when I left off my tale, the end of our trail
Had us a-hangin' there in the air.
We'd dropped so far down we could 'bout touch the ground,
So it weren't hard to dismount from there.
Although mightily frighted, I swung down and alighted.
An' I have to admit I was thrilled!
But my brave horse had plummeted thousands of feet…
So unfortunately, poor ol' Darby was killed."

And here he might sigh, and brush a tear from his eye,
Or perhaps feign a moment's confusion.
Or tug on his whiskers as he waited for his listeners
To arrive at the obvious conclusion.
And some remained hushed, while others might blush
To find themselves quite so chagrined.
Because the way he could spin it, it might take them a minute
To see how far he'd taken them in.
If they could accept his initial precept that he'd really tried to leap that cavity,
Then they'd have to concede that he'd made them believe
That he wasn't subject to gravity!
And sometimes the crowd would groan right out loud,
While the captain allowed them to dangle.
Then their pardon he'd beg if by pulling their legs,
He had caused them to stand at an angle!

And the look in their eyes when they realized
That ol' Darby had avoided disaster!
And they all gave thanks that the captain's pranks
Had turned their sorrow into laughter.

All agree that Arizona's Grand Canyon is one of God's greatest creations.
But for some it was a fitting backdrop for the "captain's" fantastic fabrications.
The depth and the breadth of its gorges is breathtaking and inspirational.
But just to watch John Hance hoodwink a tourist
Was nothing short of sensational.
Almost half the attraction of the canyon
Was to witness the "captain" pull a fast one.
And the only thing certain was that his next tall tale
Would be bigger and wilder than his last one!

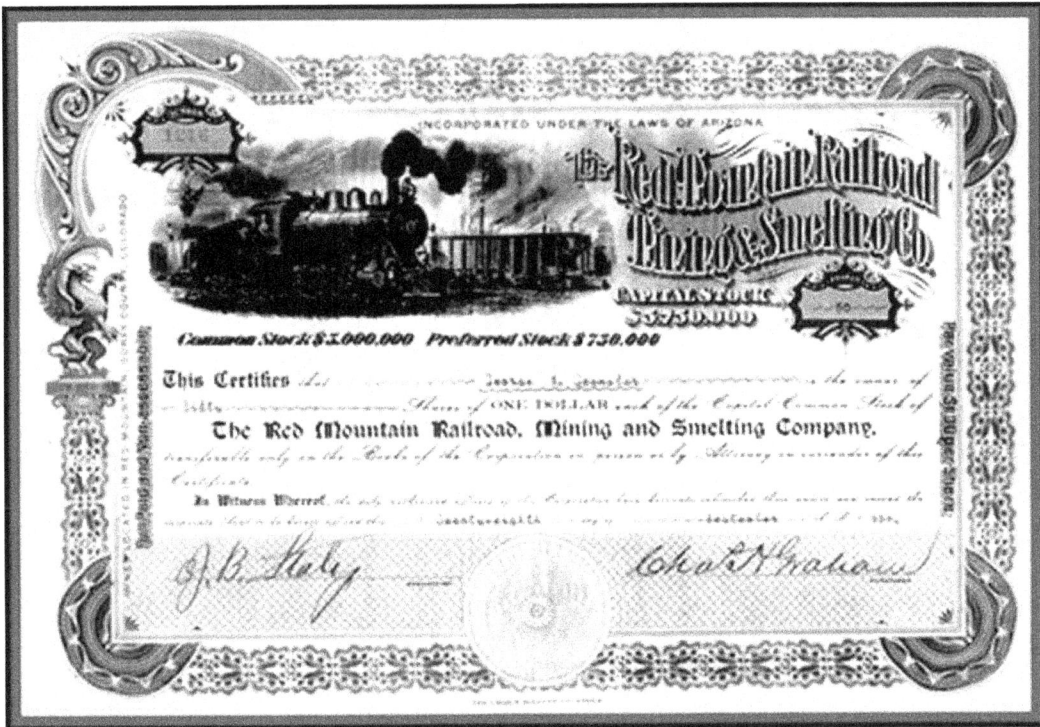

Julian's Mine

I learned of this story in Marshall Trimble's book, *Arizoniana*, in his chapter "Con Men of Yesteryear". Trimble does not give Julian's last name or the name or location of his mine, nor does he provide the names of the three Irish miners; but as he is the official Arizona State Historian it is a safe assumption he has a credible source for the story, although that is another item he does not mention.

Julian's credulity is not unique when it comes to stories of Arizona's mining history. Prospector George Warren served as the model for the miner depicted on Arizona's State Seal. He discovered the ore vein that came to be known as the Copper Queen Mine which essentially gave birth to the town of Bisbee, and produced incredible fortunes. But he lost his share of the claim in a drunken bet that he could outrun a horse. His share was valued at about $20,000 at the time (about $490,000 today). Another con man who used the name of "Doctor" Richard Flowers ran a phony mine investment scheme in an operation he called the Spendazuma mine. Marshall Trimble records that "mazuma" was a contemporary slang term for money, which would indicate that Flowers was almost taunting his victims by using a name which could be taken to mean "spend your money", but it might also be noted that the name of the fabled Aztec ruler Montezuma was much in vogue at the time. Historian William Hickling Prescott published a theory that central Arizona had been the location of Aztlan, the legendary homeland from which the Aztecs had begun their migration southward to the Valley of Mexico, and the Aztec emperor's name had been bestowed on a number of landmarks in the Territory. The name would also have been familiar to veterans of the Mexican-American War. According to legend, the phrase "from the halls of Montezuma" was incorporated into the lyrics of the Marine Corps Hymn prior to 1900. Another salting scheme discussed by Trimble concerns an 1872 fraud perpetrated by Philip Arnold and John Slack known as the Great Diamond Hoax. These hucksters used a bagful of industrial gems to lure some San Francisco bankers into setting up a ten million dollar syndicate. Although the field they'd salted was actually located in southern Colorado, the logo for their enterprise showed an ocean-going vessel, presumably laden with ore, steaming up Arizona's Hassayampa River! For a good portion of its course the Hassayampa flows underground, and legend has it that anyone who drinks its water will never again be able to refrain from lying. The syndicate's investors dispatched a representative to inspect the field, but Arnold and Slack insisted he be blindfolded when they took him there. In spite of this, Clarence King of the United States Geological Survey was able to locate the field and he quickly debunked the hoax. Arnold and Slack got away with a considerable amount of cash, but the enthusiasm for diamond hunting continued to send prospectors scouring the deserts and canyons adjacent to southwestern Colorado. As a result of all this unrewarded expenditure of energy, there is an area in far northeastern Arizona that to this day bears the moniker Diamond Fields.

JULIAN'S MINE

It didn't take long for the news to spread about the gold in Julian's mine.
His miners were painting the town bright red;
The shareholders were feeling quite fine.
The stock brokers down at the local exchange
Were busily peddling their wares.
And Julian knew it would be a wise move
If he could just buy back some of those shares.
But with the promise of dividends looming, the investors were holding fast.
And as long as that mine was booming,
Their expectations for profits were vast.
Then three Irish miners approached him,
With shares they were willing to transfer.
They knew that mine's profits were growing,
But they had no visions of grandeur.
They'd never seen the like of Julian's strike,
And the stock hadn't yet reached its prime,
But their folks back in Ireland
Depended on them,
So they couldn't gamble with time.
This new vein of gold
Was a sure motherlode,
And the speculation was brisk.
But deferred compensation
Held grave implications,
For a miner's life holds constant risk.

They knew they were selling their shares low,
But they had to meet family demands.
If God called them to heaven tomorrow,
They'd rather have the bird in their hands.
They knew it seemed crass, but they needed the cash,
So they were willing to part with their shares.
Julian was surprised, but he kept it disguised
As he gave them the papers prepared.
The transaction was quickly completed, and their shares were handed over.
So Julian got what he needed, and the miners were rolling in clover.

"Our great emancipator", those miners christened Julian.
But it was only a few days later that his fate began to turn cruel again.
He was informed by the somber-faced foreman
That the new vein had all but played out.
His senses had failed to warn him, and now he had reason to doubt.
When they'd taken him down into the tunnel, its walls had fairly glistened,
But to that voice of caution in his head, he now wished he had listened.
He'd seen how the walls of that shaft were flecked,
And to what heights his spirits had vaulted!
But now he had serious cause to suspect
That his mineshaft had merely been salted!
His heart's delight and the flickering light had blinded him to the conspiracy.
Now his credit was tight, and his shareholders' spite
Was destined to bankrupt him seriously.
His fortunes had reversed. His reputation was besmirched.
He was the victim of a criminal caper.
But worse than the curses, his stock was now worthless,
Except maybe to use as wallpaper.

But then the mine owner recalled to mind that altruistic threesome.
And he was vindictively inclined to haul them in and squeeze 'em.
He had no doubt that those Irish louts had perpetrated this scheme.
But as sure as his name was Julian, he'd prosecute those hooligans,
And justice would reign supreme.
So he had the sheriff track them down and haul them up before him.
But they maintained their innocence, and meekly they implored him.
"That someone put one over on you, it seems is undeniable.
But it wasn't us, and to prove that's true, we'll all swear to that on a Bible."
From behind his desk, Julian fetched a leather bound holy text.
And he stared the three men in the eyes to see what they'd do next.
But they placed their hands on that scripture, and swore without hesitation.
With pious pride they testified, with no sign of trepidation.
"None of us had aught to do with this nefarious deed.
As God is our judge, we'll suffer His grudge.
We swear by our Catholic creed!"
Julian told the sheriff to let them go. He'd concluded his examination.
"I know these men to be devout. They wouldn't risk damnation.
These kind of men are capable of sin, of slander and of libel.

But no good Irish Catholic would do something so drastic
As to lie with his hand on a Bible."

So the sheriff was compelled to let them go,
'Though he knew that they were roughnecks,
And to look elsewhere for clues, although he had no other suspects.
Julian left the Bible on his desk, to remind him of this lesson.
The question of who had salted his mine continued to keep him guessing.
But the longer it sat there, the more he despaired,
And the more his spirits mired.
While Julian brooded, the criminals eluded the detectives that he'd hired.
And so at length he decided it was time to return
That Bible to its place on the shelf,
But when it slipped from his grip and fell open on the desk,
He began to curse himself.

As he gazed at what was printed there, his heart was filled with rage
When he read the words "Webster's Dictionary"
Emblazoned on the title page!
Those miners had anticipated that they'd need
To protect themselves from perjury.
They'd snuck into his office and performed a deed of literary surgery!
They'd removed the Bible's pages
And found its binding pliable.
Their boss would judge this book by its cover.
And that fact had proved reliable.

The miners had made their getaway,
And they'd managed to cover their tracks.
And Julian wondered how much high-graded gold
They'd stuffed into their packs.
Down there in the dust and the darkness
They had practiced their criminal craft.
Julian thought he'd been benevolent,
But those miners were malevolent,
And they'd given their employer the shaft.
His faith in mankind had been undermined, and the truth caved in on Julian.
The world would mock. He was a laughingstock.
He'd been fooled once, and then he'd been fooled again!

When it came to judging the character of men,
He'd known some could be contrary.
But he'd never dreamed he'd be stabbed in the back
With the pages of a dictionary!
And if we ask, "Who's most at fault?" perhaps you can take your pick.
Is he whom gold makes gullible really the most culpable?
Or was it those who engineered this trick?
The eyes are the windows of the soul, and Julian thought he'd looked there.
But these men controlled what they would show,
And Julian had mistook there.
Some men have a face like an open book. You can read them at a glance.
But you can be too kind, and some will rob you blind
If you give them half a chance.
The social contract demands that we act with a modicum of modesty.
But naiveté allows some to prey on such expectations of honesty.
The miners' heist had assayed the price for this lesson he was learning.
All that glitters is not gold, so you have to be discerning.
If you were to say, "The sky is blue" to this newly-chastened Julian,
He'd be more exacting of its hue, and say, "No, I think it's cerulean."

The pursuit of wealth has admitted stealth and betrayal into human dealings.
And some have found that underground
They can hide their covetous feelings.
And 'though many a plot that was hatched in the dark
Has not seen the light of day,
Many a scheme has remained unseen, and continues to tunnel away.
And some of us, when sad, no doubt, have carelessly opined,
"How much better off my life would be, if I just had my own gold mine!"

So in the catalog of the obvious, please add this to the compendium:
Things look different on the surface than they do when you dig into them.

Expenses Out of Pocket (the Story of Bill Duckin)

This is one of the Canyon Diablo lawmen written about by Gladwell Richardson. I first came across this story in an <u>Arizona Highways</u> article about Canyon Diablo written by former Coconino County Sheriff Cecil Calvin Richardson. I cited this source in the introduction to "Ridin' to Canyon Diablo" in my book <u>The Facts Keep Gettin' in the Way of the Story</u>, mentioning that I assumed that Gladwell and Cecil having the same last name was merely a coincidence. As the old saying goes, never assume. It turns out the Richardsons were a large family, and Gladwell and Calvin were siblings.

As my poem "Gladwell Richardson and the Burden of Reputation" details, much of the "history" he wrote about has come to be questioned by current Western scholars, but given Cecil Richardson's work in law enforcement, I'm inclined to believe that his inclusion of Bill Duckin's story in his article testifies to a factual basis for the events described. But either way, I found that, whether true or not, this story lent itself nicely to the theme "Deceptions, lies and alibis sometimes worked and sometimes backfired in the Old West" which lies at the heart of many of the stories in this book.

Expenses Out of Pocket
(The Story of Bill Duckin)

Some say it's clothes that make the man. That's the haberdasher's art.
And no matter what role you've chosen in life, it helps to dress the part.
A gambler, for example, affects a certain style.
He wears the clothes he's come to know can help him with his guile.
His fancy watch and gaudy rings are chosen to impress.
He knows his livelihood depends on dressing for success.
His beaver hat and brocade vest are tailored to deceive,
And to keep his mark's attention off the aces up his sleeve.
The farmer or the rancher need garments tough and practical.
While a lawman or an outlaw have a need to be more tactical.
What's worn on the ranch or out on the farm keeps the elements at bay.
But if your hand and your gun are what keep you from harm,
You need clothes that stay out of the way.

An ex-preacher from Texas adopted an alias, he called himself Bill Duckin.
And Canyon Diablo was the nexus that he chose to try his luck in.
By way of an accessory he wore the marshal's star.
Two six-guns were a necessity he knew could take him far.
He wore a long, black frock coat not unlike an undertaker.
And many were the outlaws he dispatched to meet their maker.
Some men will keep a lucky charm, like pictures or sweethearts' lockets.
Duckin's luck was at the ends of his arms.
He kept his hands in his pockets.
And those foolish enough to try him soon learned without a doubt
That Bill did not need to draw his guns, 'cause he'd cut those pockets out.
His hands were at the ready, resting on the pistol handles.
And when he tilted those barrels up, their lives were snuffed like candles.
They might think they had the drop on him, but their chances were remote
When the bullets started flying from beneath that black frock coat.

His success in law enforcement was something of a rarity.
And collecting his own salary proved a boon to his prosperity.
When he was hired, the townsfolk pledged to provide his monthly pay.
But Bill preferred to collect their tithing every seventh day.
And the merchants didn't have much choice but to pay the extra dues,
'Cause none of them had what it took to try to fill Bill's shoes.

Bill had quit religion for a job perhaps less healthy,
But now he shepherded his new flock on a path sure to make him wealthy.
He bought himself a second suit to wear on fancy occasions.
Like when collecting for the Marshal's Fund, soliciting donations.

Bill was dressed to ensure success. He had his life all sewn up.
But that thread became unraveled on the day his plans got blown up.
He was making his collection rounds and thinking about retirement.
He wasn't sensing danger. He was comfortable in his environment.
When a challenger confronted him, and shouted, "Fill yer hand!"
Bill reacted with his usual move, but it didn't go as planned.
He let go of the money bag and thrust his gun hands down,
But that stranger's shot passed through his heart on its way out of town.
Bill's fingers couldn't find the triggers that day.
They were stopped by the fatal fact that he was wearing his good coat –
The one with the pockets intact.

Bill's luck had become entangled in fate's cruel wefts and warps.
But you'd have to give him credit – he sure made a well-dressed corpse!

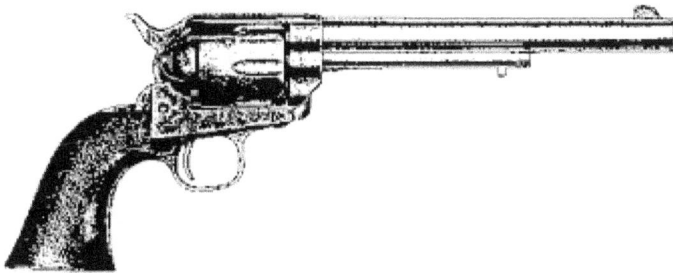

The Gunfight at Big Hat, 1893

Historian Leo W. Banks tells this story in his book, <u>Rattlesnake Blues, Dispatches from a Snakebit Territory,</u> but it is entirely made up. What is true about it, is that it was published in the *New York Tribune* on March 26, 1893. Banks goes on to note that this same story, with changes of locale, characters and ethnicities, went on to appear in various newspapers over time. For example, <u>True West</u> publisher Bob Boze Bell reports that as recently as 1939, a writer claimed that two notorious Denver madams had fought a pistol duel in Olympic Park on August 24, 1877, stripping to the waist lest their blouses should inhibit their aim! The account claims that although neither of the duelists was hit, a spectator was nicked in the neck by one of the errant bullets. (One need not look far for a moral here.) Apparently the inclusion of details like the wounded bystander, the date, location, and state of (un)dress of the participants lends enough credence that Bell notes that the story is repeated "almost annually."

The *Tribune* story is part of a tradition that Banks and others have labeled "Arizona Bashing". The Arizona Territory brought much of this bashing on itself with a lengthy record of criminal activity, range wars pitting cattle men versus sheep men, bloody military campaigns and massacres against indigenous native peoples (some of whom had allied themselves with the United States Army or had lived as peaceful neighbors of American citizens), business corruption, and political chicanery. Some Arizona newspaper editors contributed to the Territory's reputation as a place worthy of derision (see Joseph Mulhatton, and Waggin' the Dragon's Tale in this volume) by printing stories without factual verification.

As for historical reality, the accompanying Thomas Nash political cartoons (which are exceptions to the jounalistic tendencies of their day) show that Chinese who were brought to America to provide cheap labor were targets of racism in Oregon and California in addition to other parts of the West. And despite the derisive claims of the ficticious story told in this poem, Wing F. Ong was elected to the Arizona legislature in 1946, becoming the first Asian-American to be elected to public office in the continental United States. He also served a term in the Arizona Senate. Additionally, Arizona judge Thomas Tang was the first Chinese-American to serve on the federal Ninth Circuit bench.

LET THE CHINESE EMBRACE CIVILIZATION, AND THEY MAY STAY.

The Gunfight at Big Hat, 1893

A snake encountered on your path may cause you some commotion.
And sharks must be avoided if you're swimming in the ocean.
A spider's venom you may feel if careless with your fingers.
In darkened streets and alleyways the criminal often lingers.
Insulted, injured enemies are apt to be belligerent.
Against such common dangers one's accustomed to be vigilant.
But there's a desperado who might catch you without warning –
Beware the lazy writer who does newspaper reporting.

In the Old West, folks were put to the test,
But they faced the day with courage and persistence.
But they didn't have much patience for the views of unseen agents
Whose words were used to scorn them from a distance.
Reporters for Eastern newspapers portrayed them as killers and rapers,
And wrote that they were barely civilized.
Everyone west of St. Louis was filthy and ragged and shoeless,
And leaving the East was very ill-advised.

Arizonans were often maligned by reckless, caustic headlines
Composed at the approach of some reporter's daily deadline.
When sniffing out a story, news men's instincts were quite primal,
And nobody was ever safe from defamation or from libel.
Their empathy did not extend to normal social graces,
And the vitriol spewed was especially rude when directed at foreign races.
Such journalistic snobbery is apt to create a schism.
But editorial rage was seldom raised in response to such racism.
They were fond of dishing dirt at places unfamiliar.
Any place they've never been was obviously inferior.
And readers didn't much seem to care if the verbiage was uncouth.
They read it there in black and white, so it had to be the truth.

And all these faults assembled on a page of the New York Tribune
When a column described a gunfight on a main street at high noon.
Two Arizona denizens in a place they called Big Hat
Had taken offense to each other's intents and grown so angry that
Each had pulled his pistol, but to lessen their travail,
Each grabbed a passing Chinaman firmly by his pigtail.

Then the combatants blazed away, each gunman now concealed
Behind the squirming Chinamen they used as human shields!
Despite the exchange of several shots, no injuries were reported.
What passed for "honor" was satisfied, and the gun play was aborted.
The smoking guns were holstered and the pigtails were released.
The Chinese were scared, but their lives were spared —
For another hour at least!

In the rest of the article's paragraphs, there was no condemnation.
Instead the writer wondered about Big Hat's population:
Were the Chinese so abundant they were always near at hand?
And was this use spontaneous, or had it been pre-planned?
Perhaps it was so common as to have become tradition?
To practice grabbing passing ropes might save one from perdition.
But pity the overweight citizen who grabs without inspection,
And finds his Chinaman too thin to offer much protection!

Next the writer wondered if Big Hat's various residents
Had assembled and become a town because of similar precedence.
Had their views by large hats at the theater been obstructed?
And had the resulting frustration then, to this place them conducted?
Was the population united by the same abuse of fashion?
And hatred then infused in them a wild, hair-triggered passion?
And it wasn't just the Tribune that entertained such speculation;
Other papers contributed their own exaggerations:
Was it only big hats now that made them feel so furious?
Or did other fashion trends conspire to make them so injurious?
Would too much flair in western wear cause a man to be gunned down?
Fancy pants would stand no chance in such a ragged town.
Top hats and spats and silk cravats might land a man in jail.
And when hygiene demands, they wipe their hands on anyone's shirt tail.
These citizens did not care "to ape the effete ways of the East",
But did an undertaker's monkey suit dignify the deceased?
This journalistic mockery was highly entertaining.
And if it wasn't reality-based, that didn't need explaining.
Arizona was a far-away place. It was known to be wild and deadly.
And when it came to such claims of vice and shame,
Eastern readers accepted them readily.

Arizona was deserving of this kind of degradation.
Conmen, cutthroats, whores and thieves comprised its population.
Arizona's frontier was outside the sphere of modern communication,
So a reporter under pressure could look there for inspiration.
Newsmen thrived on stories they contrived about places of high mortality.
And as long as papers sold, the writing could be bold,
And not burdened by a basis in reality.

But if you search on a map for this town called Big Hat,
You're only going to end up with frustration.
For this place of daily sleaze, with its paranoid Chinese,
Exists in the twists of a journalist's imagination.
And reporters weren't content just to conjure up events,
They also must describe fitting locations.
And if the worse the better, their calumny was unfettered
When heaping filth upon their own creations.

PACIFIC CHIVALRY

And when gathered with other hacks, they'd slap each other's backs,
And engage in bouts of smoking and of drinking.
Because when beset by doubts about what they were writing about,
Fiction was often easier than thinking.

Arizonans made easy targets for the papers in Eastern markets,
So they could be attacked without redress.
And if threatened with retribution, editors cited the Constitution,
And wrapped themselves in Freedom of the Press.
And if Arizonans felt slandered by the press's lack of standards,
The protests that they made at best were feeble.
Newspapers are corporations,
And in league with the courts of this nation,
Corporations have more power than mere people.

As citizens we are slighted, and we ought to stand united,
But we cower before the power of corporations.
If we let them reign supreme, they'll infect us with their schemes,
And multiply our trials and tribulations.
Newspapers are employers, and they're staffed with corporate lawyers
Before whom righteous indignation quails.
But abuse of the Constitution is as immoral a solution,
As hiding behind innocent passing pigtails.

JUSTICE FOR THE CHINESE

The Graham County Train Robbery of 1895

Major Andrew James Doran (July 11, 1840 – February 15, 1918) first saw what would soon become the Arizona Territory as an officer in Colonel James Carlton's California Column in 1862. The first fourteen years of his post-Civil War civilian life were involved in mining and railroad building in California and Utah. He participated in the famous "Golden Spike" ceremony at Promontory, Utah where the two separately constructed sections of the nation's first transcontinental railroad were joined. In San Francisco he participated in the construction of the first railroad turntable to be used in the United States. His return to Arizona (by then a U. S. Territory) came in 1876 when he was hired to build the processing mill for the Silver King Mine, located between Globe and Florence. He became the mine's second superintendent and is credited with returning it to peak efficiency by restoring discipline and eliminating the practice of "high grading" (see Hasta la Vista, Fashionista). Faced with an increasing frequency of violent and lethal crimes, the citizens of Florence petitioned him to run for Sheriff in 1882. Doran easily won the position, but legal complications involving a case where a vigilance committee had entered the jail in his absence and hanged two of his prisoners caused him to curtail further pursuit of a career behind the badge. His leadership qualities continued to be admired by Arizona's citizens and he was elected to the Territorial Legislature six times and was twice chosen to be President of the Council. It was as a legislator that he, along with two fellow legislators, proposed the creation of the Arizona Pioneer's Home. His final pre-retirement years were spent as its superintendent. In addition to his legislative duties, Doran also served as a commissioner for Arizona's delegation to the 1893 World's Columbian Exposition, and he served as President of the Board of Managers for Arizona's presentation at the 1904 St. Louis World's Fair.

In the course of his long and productive life, Doran's list of accomplishments includes his participation in several seminal events in the formative history of the American West. Yet in spite of the gravity of his accomplishments, he was fond of recounting stories in which he himself was either the victim or a helpless bystander. In the course of his career(s), he did much traveling on stage coaches and trains in Arizona which placed him at the right place and right time to be the victim of what he described as his "annual holdup". The following is my take on one such Doran story. Even though Doran was one of the victims of the robbery, he is said to have been fond of telling this tale on himself.

I have given some embellishment to the robber's dialogue, but it is close to and true to the spirit of what was reported in the *Graham County Bulletin* in 1895.

The Graham County Train Robbery of 1895

The passengers rocked to the lullaby of sundry traveling noises,
But their slumbers were interrupted by the sound of rising voices.
Two strangers at the back of the car were engaged in conversation
As they had been ever since the train had pulled out from the station.
But now the passengers could not ignore the sound of the quarrelers' speech,
Whose decibels were rising and were audible to each.
One advocated a position that the other one assailed.
And their voices now had risen above the rhythm of the rails.

Then one of the men abruptly stood, and stepped into the aisle.
"Please give me your attention, friends," he said with a toothy smile.
"My pal and I are in need of your help in resolving a dispute.
He's voiced an opinion about the state of man that I intend to refute.
He claims no more than three men in five believe they have a soul.
So with your help, we'll prove him wrong by conducting a simple poll.
Compared to my friend, my view of mankind is definitely more cheerful.
To live a life without a soul would leave one cowed and fearful.
Without a soul, how could one hope to understand God's plan?
So if you agree and think like me, then please raise your right hand."
The stranger gave his friend a look as if to say, "See there?"
The right hand of every passenger was swaying in the air.

"That's fine, my friends," the stranger said.
"Please keep them there for a moment.
There's a second part to this dispute my pard here wants to foment.
He also maintains that nowadays no one believes in heaven or hell.
Raise your left hands to testify he's got that wrong as well."
The stranger gave a satisfied sigh, while his seated friend just glowered.
The upraised lefts next to the rights waved like a field of flowers.
The passengers looked around the car in righteous satisfaction.
And they smiled in benediction that approved each other's actions.
But on returning their gaze to the stranger, they couldn't believe their eyes –
His smile was now punctuated by a brace of forty-fives!

"We thank you, my friends," the stranger said,
"For helping to settle our bet.
You're the most obliging bunch of folks that we have ever met.

And I'm sure you're not in haste to find out if you're graced,
Or whether you are destined for the fire.
So please don't make objection while we take up our collection.
Just kindly push those hands up a little bit higher.
Any sudden moves will not be approved,
And are like to be your final – and fatal – transgressions.
But your salvation is for certain if your soul is here unburdened
From the weight of all your dross and earthly possessions.
As it says in the Good Book, it's to your soul that you should look,
And render up those things that are meant for Caesar.
If you could ask your mother, you know she'd have you do no other.
So let's not do anything that would displease her."

Then the second stranger stood, and removed their worldly goods,
And no one dared protest their being fleeced.
Because in spite of feeling harassed, if not completely embarrassed,
They'd rather be deceived than be deceased.
So the robbers made their haul, and politely thanked them all
For the generosity and passivity of their tithing.

Then they made their getaway, leaving some to pray,
Some swearing, and some with impotent anger writhing.

Now it's a proven fact that even if your life's on track,
You're still condemned to share the journey with strangers.
And some will be polite, but in spite of that they might
Present you with dilemmas or with dangers.

Some people lead a quiet life; some people crave attention.
And some will start an argument to profit from the tension.
And maybe it's essential that questions existential
Arise before we've reached our destination.
A life of too much tranquility promotes vulnerability,
And that's a path to helpless victimization.

So if called upon to judge, or to settle someone's grudge,
Or to intervene in someone else's affair,
Best keep a wary eye, for danger there may lie,
And crooked schemes may catch you unaware.
Tricks may be concealed by loud talk and righteous appeals,
Or by testimonies Biblically detailed.
So if the situation demands, before you show your hands,
Be careful, lest your plans may be derailed.

Gladwell Richardson and the Burden of Reputation

Gladwell Toney Richardson (1903-1980) came from a large family that owned and operated trading posts across the southwest under their own name as well as using the surnames Smith and McAdams. His father Samuel Richardson also owned cattle ranches in Oklahoma and Arizona. Gladwell's trading post career began at age sixteen. At seventeen, he joined the Navy for the first of two enlistments. His writing career began at age twenty-five with a series of sea adventures published in <u>Street and Smith's Sea Stories Magazine</u>, but the vast majority of his published works are in the western genre. He is credited with the publication of approximately 300 stories, novels and articles, using at least twenty-nine known pen names! One of these *nom de plumes* was John Robert Ringo which seems an obvious nod to the notorious John Peters Ringo of Tombstone fame. Richardson's use of this name is perhaps unintentionally ironic, in that the historic Ringo's reputation as a gunman has come to be somewhat suspect and questioned in works by historians and authors like Roscoe G. Willson, James A. Crutchfield, Bill O'Neal, and Dale L. Walker. Another of Richardson's pen names was *Asdzani Noodi Naalte,* (accent marks missing). *Asdzani* is sometimes given as a Navajo woman's name, while *Naalte,* according to Chic Sandoval in <u>Navajo Blessingway Singer: the Autobiography of Frank Mitchell</u>, refers to a slave captured in war. An online Navajo-to-English dictionary translates "noo" as a pit or hole in the ground, and the suffix "di" as indicating "the" or possibly "at". Granted, the placement of accent marks can change word meanings in Navajo linguistics, but still one wonders if Richardson was conscious of such meanings in choosing a name that might be construed as "the grave of the captured slave Asdzani".

This penchant for aliases seems rooted in Gladwell's personal history. Western historian John Boesseneker, in commenting on an internet article about Richardson, notes that in two separate memoirs, Gladwell claimed in one to have grown up in Arizona and in the other he claims to have grown up in Oklahoma. When questioned about the discrepancy, Gladwell claimed to have grown up in both places! Boesseneker goes on to add that, "though based in fact," most of Richardson's western articles are "heavily fictionalized." He describes Richardson's legacy as "tainted" by his having "published a great deal of folklore and fabrications and passed them off as facts," and concludes that anything written by Gladwell (or written under any of his pen names) "...should not be relied on as history. Gladwell Richardson was a story teller, not a historian, and his articles should never have been published in magazines like <u>True West</u> and <u>Real West</u>, because much of what he wrote was neither true nor real."

Mark Boardman, another western historian, notes that almost all of the articles and literature referring to Canyon Diablo written within the past half century uses much of Richardson's terminology and cites his information regarding the town's wild and deadly days, especially the number of killings. Bill Duckin(s)* for example, is claimed by Richardson to have lasted thirty days after becoming Canyon Diablo's marshal, and to have killed a man a day over the course of his tenure. Bob Boze Bell, historian and publisher of True West Magazine, mentions a Richardson claim of thirty-five Canyon Diablo killings over the course of a single year. This, he concludes, would have made the town "ten times as wild as Tombstone or Dodge City combined." Boardman observes that the extrapolation of such figures would result in "hundreds of violent deaths in (the) town over the years – and (its) Boot Hill would have been the largest in the West." Boardman also notes that gambler and gunman Luke Short (a Dodge City associate of Wyatt Earp and Bat Masterson) accused Richardson of plagiarizing his 1943 book, Ramrod for his 1951 story Short Trigger Man.

The above citations of Boesseneker, Boardman, and Bell are quoted from Bob Boze Bell's True West Blog, Wednesday, June 18, 2008. I also drew biological information about Gladwell Richardson from his listing on the Arizona Archives Online.

Gladwell may have felt justified in presenting fiction as truth as a means of responding to, and even taking advantage of, the long-standing tradition of "Arizona Bashing" (see The Gunfight at Big Hat, 1893). It has also been suggested that his exaggerations and misrepresentations were all part of a deliberate strategy to dramatize and popularize Canyon Diablo and the Two Guns Trading Post so that tourists would visit and financially benefit the Richardson family. Gladwell Richardson died in 1980, and whether his claims were deliberate falsehoods or the misconstructions of faulty scholarship, he lived long enough to see that one of the effects of his vast body of work was to lead many a western aficionado on (to use the title of one of his novels) The Trail to Nowhere. The comic book pictured here featured an article by Gladwell titled, "Mules Are Always Mules."

*Bell and Boardman give the spelling of this marshal's name as Duckins, but I have omitted the "s" in accordance with the spelling given in an Arizona Highways article about Canyon Diablo by Gladwell's brother, Cecil Calvin Richardson, a former Coconino County sheriff. (See Expenses Out of Pocket).

Gladwell Richardson and the Burden of Reputation

A mighty chasm split the earth, thirty miles from the town of Flagstaff.
A diabolical barrier that blocked the railroad's path.
Whipple named it Devil's Canyon when it caused him extra travel.
And when the A & P tried to build their bridge, their plans began to unravel.
The first bridge proved to be too short to span the canyon's breadth.
In all, ten years would be required to complete the railroad's quest.
And in that time, a town sprang up, and took the canyon's name.
A den of sin and iniquity, to which the outlaws came.
But when at last the railroad's work was done, the town was left to die.
'Til Gladwell came to Two Guns, a trading post nearby.
His father had purchased the trading post on the Navajo Reservation.
So the loyal son employed his pen to be his Dad's salvation.
Two Guns was the 1950's name for the former Canyon Diablo.
Publicity now was Richardson's game to make it a place folks would all know.
But Two Guns was a lonely place, not frequented by tourists.
So the trader aimed to spread its fame; and to make the public curious.
The Indian trade all by itself couldn't keep his family fed,
Canyon Diablo's bad reputation must be awakened from the dead.
The tiny Two Guns trading post was out in the middle of nowhere.
So Gladwell had his work cut out to make the public want to go there.
By any definition it was a place of isolation.
But Gladwell knew a useful tool. He employed exaggeration.

Gladwell Richardson was in love with words. His writings were prolific.
And he portrayed Canyon Diablo's past as morbid and sadistic.
He used a series of pseudonyms, to help his articles sell.
His stories used various pen names, but all were by Gladwell.
In a host of western magazines, he chronicled outlaw lives.
And of all the stories in one issue, he often wrote four or five.
He wrote with such authority, his readers felt assured.
Between novels and stories and articles, he published six million words.
And from this literary platform, outrageous claims he garrisoned.
'Til Two Guns seemed so wicked a place,
Tombstone looked tame by comparison.
Its daily fights and drunken nights would make most people despise it.
But Richardson had set his sights on trying to glamorize it.

Half a dozen marshals lost their lives in the town of Canyon Diablo.
And according to Gladwell Richardson, they met their fate with bravado.
The first one lasted five hours before being laid into his grave.
The most successful one lived for all of a month; another for only six days.
And hundreds of gunfighters spilled their blood in Hell Street's acrid dust.
Fourteen saloons to slake their thirst. Four brothels to slake their lust.
Four gambling halls, two dancing halls, open twenty-four hours a day.
A robbery every hour. The law was kept at bay.
Such nefarious deeds were a point of pride.
They boosted the town's reputation.
The worse the crimes, the more the renown For Richardson's creation.

It wasn't 'til after Richardson died, and Two Guns weathered to ruins,
That those with an interest in Tombstone's pride looked into Gladwell's doin's.
To the chance that Richardson's claims were true,
They played the role of skeptics.
And fans of Dodge City's wicked ways were equally dyspeptic.
A town that ate men for breakfast and where blood flowed like a fountain?
If men had died at such a rate, Boot Hill would be a mountain.
These statistics weren't supported by the cemetery's three-score graves.
And could western scholars have overlooked a place that was so depraved?

Gladwell Richardson was in love with words, and his readers were his pupils.
And when it came to promotion, the lesson he'd learned,
Was not to be hampered by scruples.
He published stories and articles about a town that was wild and furious.
But historians would later maintain that his alleged "facts" were spurious.
To leave the truth unvarnished to some is not compelling.
So it's best to be aware of what the storyteller's selling.
Gladwell's aim was to cause the fame of Two Guns to increase.
But purists of true western lore won't let it rest in peace.
Canyon Diablo today is a lonely place, with its echoes of despair.
But its claim to the crown of infamy,
And the claims Gladwell made to meet his needs,
Like the wind that blows its tumbleweeds…
May be just so much hot air.

Joseph Mulhatton

Born in Maryland about 1851, Joseph Mulhatton started his career as a traveling hardware salesman in Pennsylvania. From the outset, he seems to have taken delight in inventing stories which, once published in newspapers, would produce various effects on his readers. His initial foray into the realm of pranking the public was to print posters which advertised him as the agent of a furrier in New York, and claiming that ordinary house cats were in great demand for their furs. Readers were assured that they would receive the top market price for any and all such felines they could deliver to him in Leitchfield, Kentucky on a specified day. When Mulhatton failed to be present to purchase and take delivery, angry farmers from all over the county opened the cages and boxes in which they had transported hundreds of bewildered and unhappy cats and released them into the surrounding neighborhoods. The town was said to have been so overrun with the homeless kitties that the sheriff was forced to issue a ban on the use of shotguns as a means of eliminating them. On the other hand, it's safe to say that there probably wasn't much of a mouse problem in the town for a while.

In another early example of Mulhatton's cupidity, he filed a story claiming that a species of monkey was being imported from Africa to replace human field workers in the cultivation of hemp. He then followed up with a series of articles describing the monkeys. This is alleged to have caused some hemp plantations to dismiss some of their workers in anticipation of the arrival of the monkeys and caused a number of influential papers across the country to publish editorials taking sides as to whether or not such a thing was proper! Similar editorial scrapping occurred when he claimed that the perfectly preserved bodies of George Washington and Abraham Lincoln were to be displayed to paying customers at the Centennial Exposition in Philadelphia.

Mulhatton seems to have been keen on meteors. He claimed to have seen one strike the Earth in Indiana, and another in Texas. Curious Indiana residents, he stated, had not returned after venturing out to view the half mile of churned up ground left by the meteor's impact. The heat from the Texas meteor had allegedly destroyed all of the crops for miles around and, as Mulhatton had even specified the name of the town where the meteor fell, people traveled from hundreds of miles away and well-known universities sent professors to make on-site scientific observations. Apparently the Texans and university professors were undaunted by the question of what had happened to the missing Indiana folk.

In 1892, having heard that hell was actually a place called Arizona, Mulhatton moved to Dagger Wells and took up the life of a prospector. Despite the demands of locating, filing on, and working various claims, he continued to submit articles to the national press. Some of these concerned "oil gushers" spouting from the sands of the Sonoran Desert, proof that Spanish explorer and marathon trekker Cabeza de Vaca had camped at Casa Grande in 1530, and the good works of the Arizona Scientific Society of Florence. One of the Society's accomplishments, he claimed, was the creation of an artificial hot springs capable of curing scurvy and simultaneously responsible for preventing earthquakes that had been prophesied to completely destroy the entire region in the summer of 1899. In 1901, an article in *The Tombstone Prospector* described his idea of compressing and storing some of Arizona's heat into 4" cubes which could then be used to provide warmth in winter months, to generate power for mechanical or electric plants, or even shipped to Alaska to allow for the opening of a winter garden there.

In spite of periodic stays at the Phoenix Mental Hospital, life in Arizona's "dry heat" seems to have agreed with Mulhatton. According to the Pinal County census records, his age remained 56 from 1900 through 1911! Ironically, Joseph Mulhatton's dry wit was drowned when he attempted to cross the Gila River during one of its flood stages in 1913. His passing was mourned by the many friends he had made during his Arizona years, the countless readers who had been entertained by his hundreds of dispatches, and of course, by copy-hungry newspaper editors all across America.

Joseph Mulhatton

Some people love to stretch the truth or engage in practical jokes,
And an aged sage or a callow youth can fall for a clever hoax.
Fancy footwork, sleight of hand, ballyhoo and balderdash
Are tactics employed to harass and annoy,
And to separate marks from their cash.
Schemes and scams and old fashioned flim-flam
Are tools of the trickster's trade.
With hype and euphoria and phantasmagoria fast fortunes have been made.
But not everyone who plies these wiles has criminal intent.
Some folks just like to see their jokes immortalized in print.
But when they hand out the prize for spinning yarns
And journalistic incredulity,
One man among the rest was clearly the best
At perpetrating printed tom-foolery.
Like a modern day Herodotus ('though he didn't write in Latin),
None compare to the shenanigans and outlandish imaginin's
Described by Joseph Mulhatton.
Mulhatton had a way with words and a way of sounding logical.
He could make the patently absurd sound plausibly pedagogical.
Fantastic fables he foisted for fun upon a gullible nation,
And most editors weren't educated enough to penetrate his obfuscation.
Mulhatton had a theory that Arizona was the center of the Earth.
A leftover piece of creation's mud considered of little worth.
Seeing no place to put it, God pondered for a spell,
Then stuck it on the west coast of America and said,
"This place shall be called hell."
What made him think that Arizona was on the shores of the Pacific?
His geographical understanding was something less than prolific.
So he journeyed to Los Angeles in search of the devil's domain,
But he was told that he'd have to travel inland to find such accursed terrain.
And when at last he arrived on the stage in the town of Dagger Wells,
He found the landscape lent itself to fantasy and bagatelles.
Mulhatton had a fertile mind, and he'd found his inspiration.
And now the two of these entwined to fuel his observations.
He had a journalistic style so logically presented,
That it was hard to muster doubt about what he'd invented.

One of his early missives, which caused some jaws to drop
Was the story of a Tucson passenger train that had not been able to stop.
There were thousands of grasshoppers covering the tracks,
And it made the rails so slick,
That the train slid clear to Maricopa, before its brakes would stick.
The Eastern public accepted as fact these insect lubrications,
But Mulhatton hadn't mentioned that a hundred miles
Separated those two train stations.
Mulhatton had a storyteller's gift, and a talent for prevarication.
The dispatches he filed from out in the wild weren't subject to verification.

He wrote about an epic battle, in which 10,000 wild boars
Were slaughtered by an army of hunters near the Colorado River's shores.
The field of carcasses was so thick the hunters were complaining.
They were forced to climb up mountains of pigs to shoot the ones remaining.
You'd expect such reporting to raise some doubts, but you would be mistaken.
Even though the story was excessively gory, it bolstered the market for bacon.
Of those who made their living off the printing press,
There were followers and leaders.
And Mulhatton placed no restrictions on the outright fictions
That he fed to the nation's readers.

And then in 1899, with tongue firmly in cheek,
He penned a piece of reportage
That remains completely unique.
He claimed that the town of Florence
Was surrounded by a magnetic belt.
And to unwary passers-by
It made its presence felt.
The excess charge was channeled
By the fields of towering cactus.
And those who dared to pass too close
Could find these giants fractious.
One traveler met his grisly fate
When a negatively-charged saguaro
Attracted his positive state of mind.
Now he'll never see tomorrow.

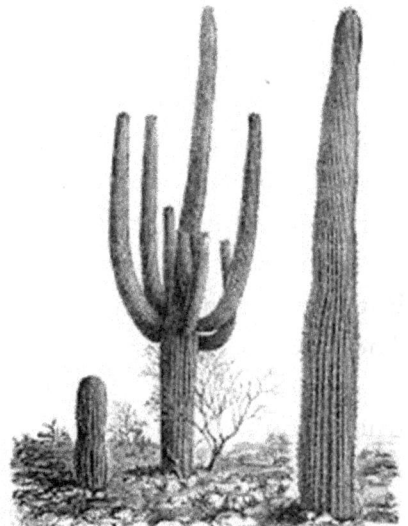

Its giant arms embraced him, and absorbed him into its folds.
Who knows how many such victims this saguaro forest holds?
Another tourist was impaled while wandering these southern latitudes
When a positively-charged saguaro prevailed
In rebuffing his negative attitude.
Any extreme modalities were something these cacti scorned.
And those with magnetic personalities were particularly forewarned.
Mulhatton feared no repercussions
From his readers' understanding of magnetism.
When it came to science he knew their compliance
Was assured by basic pragmatism.
He employed a loose interpretation when he dealt with the laws of nature.
And this story's effects might even have been felt
In the Territorial Legislature.
One wonders what percentage of readers perceived
The story's botanical hilarity,
And if it made politicians shy away from issues of strong polarity?
Mulhatton was a literary hero, a champion of the Fifth Estate.
He purveyed his distortions in measured proportions
That readers could appreciate.
He doled out mendacity mixed with sagacity that denied repudiation,
And his exaggerations fed the public's fascination
With a smattering of sophistication.
He concocted his fictions with so much conviction
That even if one could see through,
The world would seem tame and it would be a darn shame
If they turned out not to be true.

So if there's a heavenly press corps that engages in pontification,
Or an eternal tourism officials choir that sings in exaltation,
Or any angelic real estate agents that gather in convocation,
If they're from Arizona, they would have to be a Jonah
To withhold their approbation.
For if there's one chap who put that place on the map,
And that's the subject about which we're chattin',
It's a pretty safe bet they acknowledge their debt
To the stories of Joseph Mulhatton.

How Cyclone Bill Got His Name

According to author Charles D. Lauer, as a young man William Ellison (Abe) Beck, a.k.a. "Cyclone Bill" studied law and had a short-lived legal career in Texas. He and his equally young partner had been assigned by a judge to defend a man accused of stealing cattle, but when the defendant was introduced to his court-appointed counsel, he turned to the judge and said, "I plead guilty." Beck is said to have left both the courtroom and Texas, and moved west.

Beck's left knee was crippled (he claimed a shotgun blast was responsible) and caused him to limp noticeably. Historian Leo W. Banks reports that Beck was implicated in the infamous Wham Paymaster robbery of May 11, 1889, accused by Major Joseph Washington Wham of being one of the robbers. Additionally, Lauer reports that one of the soldiers in Wham's detail testified that he recognized Beck's distinctive limp in the way one of the robbers had moved from one location to another during the attack. However, Marshal W. K. Meade was forced to release him when the testimony of reliable witnesses proved sufficient for his alibi. Coverage of the trial in the *Arizona Citizen* of June 6, 1889 reported that "Mr. and Mrs. Tidwell of Eagle Creek, eighty-five miles from the scene of the robbery, swore positively that 'Cyclone' had come to their home on Friday, May 10th, and remained there until the forenoon of May 12th, and went from there to Morenci... On this testimony the defendant was discharged."

Despite his gimpy left leg, Beck traveled widely throughout the Arizona Territory and made many friends before arriving in Clifton, which became his surrogate home. During an election for Justice of the Peace, some of Beck's associates in Clifton got him approved as a write-in candidate. So many people voted for him that at first count, it appeared as though he had won the office. However, the election commission decided to disqualify any ballots that did not have the candidate's proper name written-in. One of the ballots read simply "Cyclone", another was marked, "Tornado William", and eleven others were cast for "Cyclone Bill". With these thirteen ballots disqualified, Beck's opponent, Abe Boyles, won the election by three votes. Given that Beck was also known to sometimes go by "Abe", it is lucky for Boyles' supporters that no ballots were cast with only that name written in.

There are, according to Charles D. Lauer, multiple versions as to how Cyclone Bill got his name. Leo W. Banks, writing about the Wham Paymaster robbery in Manhunts and Massacres, Arizona Highways Wild West Collection, Volume 2, cites the version in which Beck is alleged to have struck someone over the head with the leg of a cow, his victim subsequently saying that he felt as if he'd been hit by a cyclone. I have constructed my poem using the version cited by Lauer in his Tales of Arizona Territory. This version is also cited by Bob Boze Bell on his True West website. I don't know if there is a version attributing the name to Beck having been considered a blowhard by his contemporaries, but given that he is said to have taken pride in having been accused of being one of the perpetrators of the Wham Paymaster robbery, it wouldn't surprise me to learn that some contemporaries credited it to this aspect of his nature.

Holding Up the Pay Escort, by Frederick Remington

How Cyclone Bill Got His Name

Exaggeration prevails when twisted tales are claimed to be true as gospel.
And not to believe is sometimes perceived as an act overtly hostile.
W.E. Beck was a con man whose legs made an uneven pair.
And his claim that he rode a tornado snatched an alibi right out of the air.
He had partnered with a new-made acquaintance
In a bid to deliver some freight.
But on the road between Yuma and Tucson, Apaches were lying in wait.
The goods would be fetching top dollar,
But the enterprise was fraught with much danger.
But in exchange for a share of the profits,
Beck agreed to be the business arranger.
His partner supplied the goods and the wagon,
Equipped with a ten-mule team.
Beck's part would be knowingly risking his life,
To help them accomplish their dream.

So he headed the wagon for Tucson, but he vanished for over a year.
While his anguished partner in Yuma, reconciled to the worst of his fears.
He smarted from the loss of his money, but in spite of material strife,
He counted himself as quite lucky – he still had his hair and his life.
In time he could recoup his losses, but none of his blood had been spilled.
But poor Beck had lost all his resources.
He was certain Beck must have been killed.

Sometime later, while on business in Tucson,
Some goods he stepped out to inspect.
When who should come limping down Main Street –
His supposedly dead partner, Beck!
Relief quickly gave way to anger. Beck had stolen his outfit and team!
He demanded Beck make restitution. His vexation was just and extreme!

Beck said, "Now you just hold your horses. I'm a victim of strange circumstance.
I was almost half way back from Tucson,
When the weather played a curious chance.
A twister swept down on the wagon, and snatched it straight up in the air!
It spun me in dizzying circles, then flung me to earth God knows where!

I landed quite hard on my noggin. For two days my eyes saw things double.
That tornado stripped off all my clothing,
And left me with nothing but trouble.
What became of the team and the wagon? I haven't the foggiest clue.
But I remembered the direction I'd come from,
So there was only one thing I could do.
I walked all the way back to Tucson. It's a miracle I somehow survived.
And amazingly my ol' partner has found me –
I've only just this minute arrived!"

His incredibly fantastic story (for which he offered no proof),
And remarkably devoid of details, was submitted as self-evident truth.
Ol' Beck found the best way to spin it when caught with his hand in the till.
And from that day ever after, he was known by the name "Cyclone Bill."

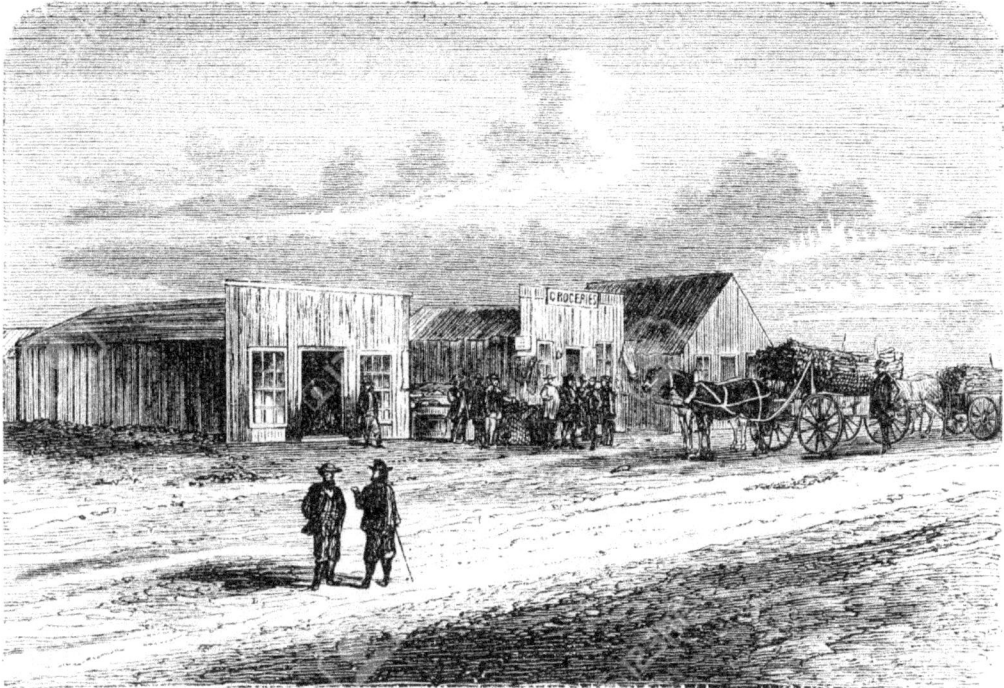

Drinks on the House
(Another Cyclone Bill Story)

This seems to be one of the better known Cyclone Bill anecdotes. It is commented on by several Arizona historians. As noted in the introduction to the previous Cyclone Bill poem, W. E. Beck's legs were of different lengths. When standing on his right leg he was above average height (some sources have put it around six feet, two inches) but when resting on the left leg he appeared to be a much shorter man. I encountered one source that said he appeared to be a dwarf when in this posture!

Another Cyclone Bill anecdote reported by Charles D. Lauer concerns a time when Judge Fletcher M. Doan was holding court in Solomonville. The judge was visited by a friend from a more civilized part of the nation and while showing him around the town, they encountered Beck at the Palace Saloon. The judge introduced Cyclone by his nickname to which Beck responded by raising himself to his full height and indignantly stating, "I'll give you to understand, sir, that my name is W. E. Beck!"

The judge, perhaps somewhat abashed, replied that he just assumed that since he was popularly known as "Cyclone Bill", he would want to be introduced as such.

To this Beck is said to have retorted, "You are popularly known around here as a first class son of a bitch, but I don't think you would want to be introduced as such!"

(This is not a picture of Cyclone Bill.)

Drinks on the House

Cyclone Bill was always a roamer,
But he hailed from the mining town of Clifton.
And the fact one leg was shorter than the other,
Was a tool that he used in his griftin'.
One night when the saloon was quite crowded,
And the new bartender was distracted,
Beck stood down on his short leg,
Which made him look much more compacted.
He caught the bartender's attention, and he acted as meek as a mouse.
But in a voice that reached every corner, he said,
"A round for everyone in the house!"

The bartender's face looked delighted, and the bar was immediately mobbed.
That fat tab made that barkeep excited.
(He didn't know he was about to be robbed.)
While the barkeep was busy with his bottles,
Cyclone Bill stepped back into the crowd.
But now he stood up on his good leg,
Which made him look quite tall and proud.
When all of the drinks had been given,
And the bartender came for his money,
Those who knew Beck just stood there a-grinnin',
But the barkeep didn't think it was funny.
The bartender had noted a short man, but he hadn't paid heed to his face.
And at the request of this diminutive stranger,
He gave drinks to everyone in the place!
The bartender never caught on to the scam,
And all he could say was, "This stinks!
Where's that sorry little sawed-off runt who owes me for all of those drinks?"

In those days when men made a bargain,
It was backed by the worth of one's word.
And on the strength of this "gentlemen's agreement"
The success of Beck's scams was assured.

Beck taught that barkeep a lesson –
'Though it might have been hard for him to swallow it –
Honest men will always honor a custom,
But dishonest men never will follow it.
If the barkeep had been more experienced,
He might not have fallen for the stunt.
But when liquor's involved in the business,
You had best get your money up front.
Most men prize their good reputations,
So they'll keep their behavior in check.
But some prey on fools and play by their own rules –
Those men like ol' W.E. Beck.
The glue that holds society together is trust and respect and good will.
But some men treat the law hell-for-leather.
So keep an eye out for the likes of Cyclone Bill.

(This is another picture that is not Cyclone Bill.)

Hasta la Vista, Fashionista

In <u>The Residents of Tombstone's Boot Hill</u>, Author Ben Traywick refers to the July 24, 1880 killing of T. J. Waters as "foremost among Tombstone tales of gun violence." Quite a claim, considering the violence that was to erupt next to Fly's Photography studio a little more than a year later. Leo W. Banks says in <u>Rattlesnake Blues, Dispatches from a Snakebit Territory</u> that T.J. Waters was a gambler. In its account of this affair, the *Tombstone Epitaph* described Waters as "what is considered a sporting man." Traywick states that Waters had been gambling earlier that day, and had apparently won an amount of money that put him in a mood to spend. He spent some of it on his new shirt, and a fair amount of it on liquor, drinking enough to become "evil tempered" and "very abusive". Both Banks and Traywick note that Bradshaw and Waters were friends. Traywick describes them as "close friends having prospected together and lived in the same cabin for a number of months." Bob Boze Bell refers to Waters as a foreman in one of his True West Moments. (Bell's title for this particular True West Moment, "That shirt was to die for", was my inspiration for writing this poem.) Multiple sources, including the *Epitaph*, quote Waters as claiming to be "the chief". It seems that in order to get by, many people in Tombstone worked at a variety of occupations. "There is not always a single truth in historical accounts," as Evelyn Howell, editor of <u>Tombstone Chronicles, Tough Folks, Wild Times</u> writes in her introduction to that volume. "What may seem contradictory cannot always be assumed to be wrong, especially when the topic is Tombstone."

While I have kept the story inside Corrigan's Alhambra Saloon, Traywick says that after Bradshaw left, Waters also left and made another circuit of the saloons along Allen Street, engaging in more arguments as he went. When he returned to the Alhambra, Bradshaw, now armed with his pistol, was watching from across the street and intercepted him at the door. It was there that Bradshaw shot Waters. Given the number of witnesses to Waters' behavior that day, and the fact that Waters had instigated the violence, Bradshaw was released after the inquest. Bradshaw would be found shot dead behind the Oriental Saloon about one year later, having made the mistake of being the boyfriend of Blond Mollie, the woman to whom gunman Buckskin Frank Leslie had taken a fancy. It appears that Leslie had settled their rivalry in the same manner in which Bradshaw had chosen to settle his dispute with Waters.

The practice of "high-grading" referred to in this poem (and in Julian's Mine) was a plague to mine owners in the early days. Miners would steal particularly valuable nuggets of ore (those of the highest grade), conceal them in bags hidden inside their clothing, and later sell or transfer them to a confederate who would then assay and sell the ore and bank the proceeds. Artist Bill Ahrendt executed a drawing that perfectly captures the essence of this practice. It is published in <u>Arizona Highways Magazine</u>, March, 1985. This practice could explain why despite the dozens of years and lives lost in searching for it, the legendary Lost Dutchman's gold mine has never been found. If Jacob Waltz, the Dutchman who claimed to have discovered and worked the alleged mine, was in fact a high-graders' agent, then the mine probably was nothing more than a fiction concocted to cover up the illicit activities of Waltz and his cohorts.

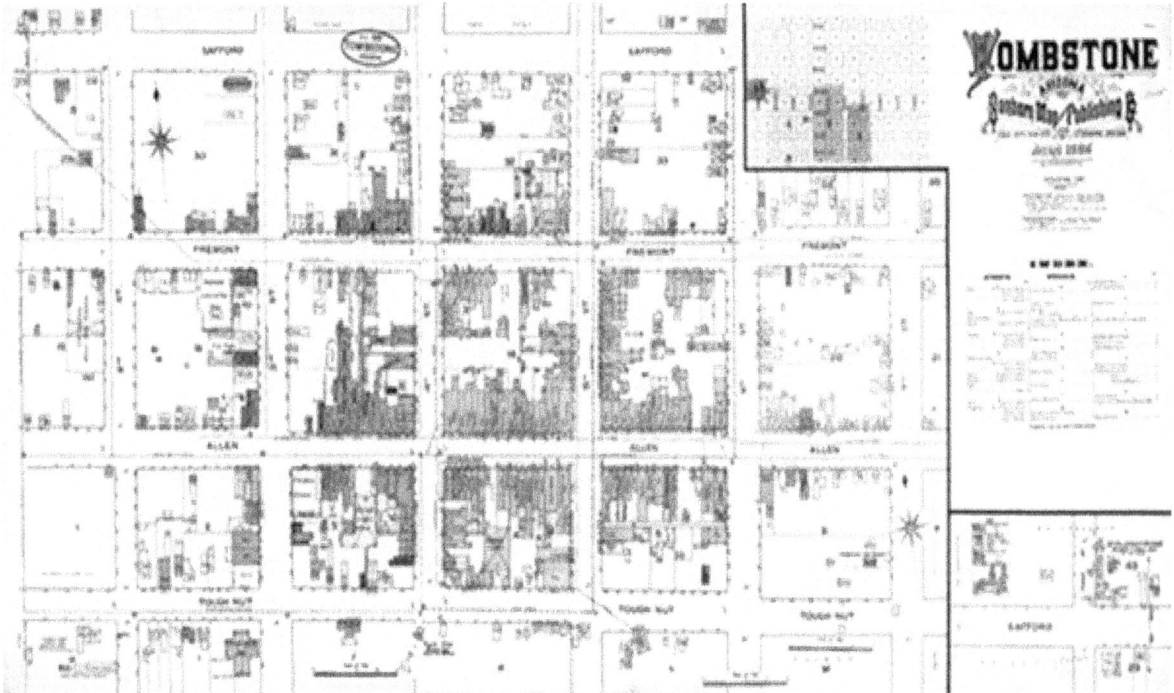

"Hasta la Vista, Fashionista"

There's not a lot of light down there in the mines
To show your fancy duds off.
You need clothes that hold up to a weekly wash
To scrub the mud and the dust off.
Plain clothes are fine when you spend your time
Stuffing dynamite into sockets.
'Though you might sew some bags inside your pants,
To help you line your pockets.
But a hard-rock miner's got no call for sashaying or parading.
But he'll make alterations he knows will pay off,
If engaged in a little "high-grading".
But he's got no need for fancy clothes until he's made his pile.
Or until the Lord snuffs out his light, and they lay him out in style.

Those Tombstone miners were pounding them down
In Corrigan's on that hot July night.
They were knocking them back and cutting the dust,
And carousing with all of their might.
God knows that a man builds a powerful thirst
Busting rocks while he's wishing for whiskey.
And now that the alcohol flowed through their veins,
They were feeling rambunctious and frisky.
Most of these men had come straight from their shifts.
You could tell by the grime on their faces.
But their foreman, Tom Waters, had washed off the grit
From most of the obvious places.

But what could not be ignored was a fashion *faux pas* –
That brand new shirt he was wearing.
An unusual style for a man of the mines,
And it had those men gawking and staring.
They weren't shy about sharing their opinions,
And they made him the butt of their kidding.
They laughed and they joked, they pointed and poked.
They gave him one heck of a ribbing.
But Waters was losing his patience. He was starting to get downright mad.

He was angered by this faction's reaction
To his shirt of bold black and blue plaid.
The veins at his temples were throbbing.
He was struggling to hold down his bile.
He would dish out some shiners to these philistine miners
If they didn't stop mocking his style.
So he drained off the rest of his whiskey,
And slammed down the empty shot glass.
"The next piece of dirt that makes fun of this shirt,
I'm gonna knock flat on his ass!
You boys like your denim and canvas, well, you're all gonna look pretty sad,
Because I'll break some necks if you don't show respect –
You'd best stop making fun of this plaid!"
So the men all changed their demeanor.
Because their boss had made them believe
He'd give them a thrashin', because when it came to fashion,
Tom Waters wore his heart on his sleeve.
But just when things had got quiet, E.L. Bradshaw came sauntering in.
And callous and curt, he remarked that that shirt
Had been tailored to make the whores grin.
Waters rose up in a fury and he smashed Bradshaw right in the face.
Staggered and bleeding, Bradshaw kept retreating,
'Til he'd backed himself out of the place.
Waters went back to his drinking. He was muttering into his glass,
"I'm their boss. I'm the chief, and I won't take no grief
Just 'cause they don't appreciate class!"
He was trying to drown his emotions.
He'd thought Bradshaw was different from the others.
Now his feelings were hurt because his plaid shirt
Had made Bradshaw show his true colors.
Waters was sullen and sulky. Bradshaw had not apologized.
So he should consider himself lucky
That he hadn't blackened both of his eyes!
Just then Bradshaw was standing behind him.
His swollen, bruised eye was still bleeding.
"Waters, you rat! Why did you do that?
I gave you no cause for a beating!"

Waters just sat there and ignored him. He'd had about all he could take.
But keeping his back turned to Bradshaw
Was the biggest mistake he could make.
Bradshaw pulled out his pistol, and 'though he was no fashion expert,
He redesigned that fabric as his bullets played havoc,
Ripping four bloody holes through that shirt.
Waters made a statement in the bar that night,
But to Bradshaw, that damned shirt was an eyesore.
In a world without compassion,
Best not turn your back on fashion,
Because in the end that plaid shirt was to die for.

Don't Judge a Book by Its Cover

I wrote this piece after musing on the lyrics to the well-known western ballad, The Streets of Larado, or A Cowboy's Lament. The song expresses a young cowboy's regrets for the choices he's made that have led to his immanent death, so it's rather sad. But the Smothers Brothers did a clever parody of it back in the 1960s:

"I see by your outfit that you are a cowboy."

"I see by your outfit that you're a cowboy, too."

"We see by our outfits that we are both cowboys. If you get an outfit, you can be a cowboy, too!"

The phrase "All hat and no cattle" inspired cartoonist Gary Doonesbury to represent President George W. Bush in the pre-Iraq war years of his administration as an empty, talking cowboy hat. After the invasion of Iraq, Doonesbury replaced this icon with an empty, talking – and ever-deteriorating – Roman centurion's helmet. Ever since the famous televised Kennedy-Nixon debates, we have insisted that any candidate hoping to occupy our nation's highest office must "look presidential". The adage that an actor must always "look the part" can be traced back to the theatrical traditions of the ancient Greeks, as illustrated in Aristophanes' *The Frogs*.

As a long-time interpreter of cultural and natural resources and back country guide, I'm familiar with the slight sense of embarrassment that accompanies the first days of wearing a new pair of boots or a new hat in front of clients. I once found my archaeology mentor sitting on his brand new hat. "I don't like to wear a hat until it has that 30 mission crush," he explained. As a professional storyteller specializing in tales from western history, I like to dress in a manner that conveys to my audiences that I'm familiar with the traditions and the lifestyles of the characters I embody. My ensemble usually includes a pair of ropers that were a gift from my wife many years ago. They are of that well broken-in condition that is not only comfortable for long hours of wear, but also gives me a sense of confidence in spite of the fact that the only cow or horse droppings they've ever stepped in has been purely accidental. Once, as I took the stage and prepared to begin my performance, I heard a gentleman in the front row turn to his wife and say, "Look at the soles of those boots. This guy obviously knows what he's talking about." We are truly a nation obsessed with appearances.

Don't Judge a Book by Its Cover

They say, "Don't judge a book by its cover."
Experience should teach us not to doubt it.
If we don't investigate its pages,
We're never going to know the truth about it.
Just 'cause the shoe fits, don't mean you should wear it.
Only human beings can change their tracks.
And what you see while staring in a mirror, is only a reflection of the facts.
We try to cloak our ill-fitting illusions, and cover up our own profanities,
But life will often make its own intrusions, exposing all our naked vanities.
A man can have meticulous precision, and carefully attend to his attire.
But all it takes is just one bad decision
To leave him lying bleeding in the mire.
In spite of our illustrious pretensions,
Or how far up the ladder we may climb,
Our fate may not comply with our inventions.
So put your pants on one leg at a time.
And if you change your morals to suit the fashion,
You'll never know how it feels to be relaxed.
A man's worth isn't measured by his wardrobe.
It's measured by the way he thinks and acts.

So if you hold a hand you think is winnin',
Good sense should tell you that you shouldn't shout it.
And even when you're wrapped up in white linen,
We'll still see that you're a cowboy by your outfit.

Some Days the Bear Eats You

This story is based on an anecdote told by Earl Van Deren in William Howard's <u>Tales of Sedona, Then and Now</u>. The gist of the story is true. The Verde cowboys told Bert New that a fight had occurred between a longhorn bull and a bear when in fact the fight was between two bulls, and Bert left the round-up soon after. I have embellished the parts about the bear seeking revenge, the taunting of Bert New, and Bert's career as a writer and lecturer. As far as I know, he never wrote anything beyond the article that Earl mentions was printed in the *Coconino Sun* newspaper. I don't know if Walt, Lloyd, and Greene reacted as I've described, but the part about the story's effect on people's curiosity is true in that Earl, who was not personally involved in these events (which happened years before the publication of Howard's book), claims that people continued to ask him about the story for many years. The Van Derens and Thompsons are two of the Verde Valley's "first families". Lloyd Van Deren's parents arrived in the Verde in 1875, and Greene Thompson's father, J. J. "Jim" Thompson, became the first Anglo settler in Oak Creek Canyon in 1876.

The phrase "to see the elephant" dates to the early nineteenth century and is often associated with military or combat experience. Wordorigins.org gives a definition of "world-weary experience." But in latter nineteenth century America it became linked with westward migration and exploration. Its meaning evolved into a way of describing the pull that the West and its seemingly limitless possibilities and fantastical reputation exerted on many people. The West was a place where one could expect to encounter strange and bizarre things. So in the vernacular it became a more colorful way to say "to satisfy one's curiosity."

In his book, <u>Billy King's Tombstone</u>, C. L. Sonnichen relates yet another example of the Eastern media's penchant for western hyperbole (see The Gunfight at Big Hat, 1893), noting that in 1882 the *Tombstone Epitaph* reprinted a story which had appeared in the *Missouri Republican* in 1879, claiming that one 4th of July a traveling circus came to town but was denied a permit to exhibit its acts within the Tombstone city limits. The show set up a couple of miles outside of town and many residents turned out for the show. The quality of the acts and exotic animals was disappointing in the extreme, prompting some of the disgruntled customers to "shoot up the show". The circus personnel fled, and the townsfolk released the animals and took possession of the elephant. It was kept in the care of the chief of the fire department, and used to lead parades through town. At such times, men mounted on its back would shoot out lights and windows with their pistols.

Sonnichsen reports that this fanciful story actually has some basis in truth. A disappointing circus did set up outside of Tombstone, and was not well-received. While the keeper's attention was elsewhere, a man named George Osborn stole the elephant and led it on a stroll down the length of Allen Street. The local citizenry were greatly amused, even though no shots were fired. Upon discovery of the theft, the circus personnel recovered their animal, packed up their tent, and left the area. So at least in this one instance, an Eastern visitor to Tombstone could say that he or she had gone out west and – literally – "seen the elephant".

Some Days the Bear Eats You

When dudes come out west, the thing they like best
Is playing cowboy for their own entertainment.
But the hard-working hands can lay their own plans
To reciprocate on that arrangement.
For one of the joys of some real cowboys is putting one over on dudes,
Spinning tall tales, blowing wind in their sails, or adopting profane attitudes.

Once a greenhorn showed up from the City of New York
In the aftermath of the First World War.
And getting in touch with the cowboy life was what he was hankering for.
He'd survived Europe, now a rope and a stirrup
And a good horse would be more relevant.
And with hope in his breast he'd headed out West
In order "to see the elephant".
So he joined any roundup that he could find
In the red rock canyons and buttes.
Wearing spurs that he had welded on to a pair of his old army boots.
And in a nod to the spirit of irony, this tenderfoot's name was Bert New.
And when he attached himself to a bunch from Oak Creek,
Some mischief was bound to ensue.

Now it happened that while riding the range one day,
Lloyd Van Deren, Greene Thompson, and Walt Baker
Had discovered a scene of cow carnage,
Where two bulls had met their maker.
A long horned bull is a belligerent beast; a truly irascible animal.
And when two square off in a dominance duel,
Their anger is practically flammable.
(But we shouldn't be too hasty to regard them with scorn.
Nature dealt a tough hand to their gender.
If your stuff was dangling just inches from thorns,
It might put you in a bad temper.)
In a thicket of manzanita, two huge bulls had engaged in a battle.
The inevitable cause for such fighting, of course,
Has to do with the female cattle.
It looked like they'd probably fought all day long,
And they'd ripped one another asunder.

The clash of their horns must have sparked like the lightning;
Their bellows must have echoed like thunder.
Copious amounts of their blood had been spilled,
And their hides were so pierced and gouged,
It was all Lloyd and Greene and Walt could do
Just to recognize that they'd been cows.

Then one of the three got inspired, and he said,
"Why gents, this is wonderfully rare!
Let's tell that greenhorn Eastern man
That this fight was between a bull and a bear!
Just give the scavengers a couple of days
And these bones will get scattered about.
And I'll lay even money that if you back my play,
Our New man won't figure it out."

Now as far as entertainment goes, this wager might seem pretty tame,
But the routine of a drive can be boring, so the boys all threw into the game.
Nowadays we're more inclined to try to be kind
And to show our veterans respect,
But when Walt, Greene and Lloyd started spinning this yarn,
No one else was about to object.
They didn't think it was cruel to play Bert for a fool
In the name of providing amusement.
'Cause when cowboys get bored hurt feelings are ignored,
And they'll join in without much inducement.
Since men took to the saddle to start herding cattle,
Cowboys have been an exclusive fraternity.
And if it's action you're chasin', you should expect that some hazin'
Will go on from now 'til eternity.

They even made a plan for what they would say
If Bert greeted their story with scorn:
"I'll tell you what, sir, it takes a mighty big bear,
To take that much bull by the horns!
Our local ursine is a murderous kind.
And that bear's mate is likely unhinged.
If you hold your life dear you had better keep clear.
That bear's widow will be seeking revenge.
She'll be haunting that spot 'til her mate's body rots.

Bear marriage is a serious vow.
So don't dare to transgress, 'cause that place will mean death
For anything that even smells like a cow.
The curious sight of that savage fight
Will stick with us for the rest of our lives.
But you'd better take care and stay the heck away from there,
'Cause a she-bear's got claws just like knives.
There are not many men who have come back again
After viewing a scene of such slaughter.
But you're not of that stamp, so just stick close to camp,
'Cause that canyon won't be safe 'til we've shot her."

Bert had branded himself with a bull's eye
When he said he was seeking adventure.
And he might have fit in if he'd been among kin.
'Least been subject to gentler censure.
Any cowpoke can be the butt of a joke
When the prospects for fun are so meager.
But as an outsider Bert had made that gulf wider
When he'd come off a trifle too eager.
So the boys played their trick and they laid it on thick,
Casting many a slight and aspersion.
Until just like the cows, Bert was thoroughly choused
'Til his hackles were ruffled for certain.

The next morning's fire found a rollicking choir
Of laughter over coffee and biscuits.
There were salutations and congratulations on ridding themselves of a misfit.
The word went around Bert was nowhere to be found.
He had packed up his kit and vamoosed.
And Walt, Lloyd and Greene were all seen as quite keen
At scaring off unwanted recruits.

But it wasn't much later that a Flagstaff newspaper
Ran a story under Bert New's byline
About red rock trails, and full of lurid details
About a duel between a bear and a bovine!
Bert it seems had abandoned his dreams of being a red rock range rider.
He'd traded that obsession for the loftier profession

Of becoming a famous western writer!
And those cowboys groused, and said Bert couldn't vouch
For the accuracy of the "facts" that he was selling.
But it turned out Bert was blessed while on this trip out West
When he got taught the art of storytelling!
A landscape so ethereal provided raw material,
And his imagined exploits always went unquestioned.
And the cowboys were horrified when by the public he was glorified
As a chronicler of western folklore, myth and legend.
His fictional experiences got him many paid appearances
At venues on the national lecture circuit.
Those boys thought that they had tripped him,
But their story had equipped him
With the means to make his living – he could work it!

And even years later, some visiting agitator
Would ask to be shown that bloodied battle ground.
Because Bert's publicity lent authenticity
As that story kept making the rounds!
And as time went by, Walt, Lloyd, and Greene would sigh,
And regret their prevarication.
And they felt like jerks when at their honest work
They were pestered for verification.
Tourists peppered them with questions, and asked for directions,
Interrupting them ad infinitum.
And it made them choke that such a harmless little hoax
Could keep coming back around to bite 'em.
They were not built to be nagged by the guilt that was theirs by association.
Sad and forlorn they were caught
On the horns of a dilemma
Of their own creation.

So if you're ever up on the Red Rock range,
Just know that you'd best be prepared
To hear wild claims
That are weird and strange
Just to test whether or not you'll get scared.
Those good ol' boys may hoot and make noise
To see how far your leg they can pull.
Show them what you can bear, just act devil-may-care,
'Cause they're prob'ly just throwing some bull!

The Lady with the Lethal Lingerie

This story was reported by Bill Roberts in his much-missed newspaper, *The Jerome Traveler*, in an article titled, Sheriff Has "Mad" Time in 1909. Because many of Arizona's early towns came into being in association with male-dominated industries like mining, ranching, railroading, and military service, there was a tolerance for "the world's oldest profession" and many towns and cities had ordinances specifying the minimum proximities allowed between such designated establishments and any nearby schools or churches. But as churches gained greater influence, and as more and more women, including wives and daughters, came to reside in these towns, greater pressure was exerted on city fathers to increase these distances and ultimately to outlaw prostitution as a sign of having attained a higher level of civilization. But for many women of the early West, prostitution represented a last resort by which they might, in the aftermath of losing the support of a husband due to incarceration, death, divorce, or abandonment, remain relatively free and self-sufficient. The alternative of returning to their hometowns often meant spinsterhood and/or enduring the scorn of disapproving relatives and neighbors. And while a few might have actually earned enough income to retire or purchase a more dignified life for themselves elsewhere, many succumbed to the occupation's often fatal associations with alcoholism, drug addiction, and violence. The satirical tone of my poem is in no way intended to minimize the plight of those who, in spite of our modern pretenses to civilization and humane social policies, find themselves caught up in these same cycles of desperation.

HOSIERY.

Ladies' Silk Hose.

NOVELTIES IN LADIES' FANCY COTTON
AND LISLE THREAD HOSIERY.

The Lady with the Lethal Lingerie

Arizona was becoming civilized in the early twentieth century.
But plenty of money was still to be made with liquor and with wenchery.
Ada Ferrara met Ashfork's demands for sex and inebriation.
And she believed in that business mantra – location, location, location.
Ada knew that she could keep the competition behind her
As long as it was easy for her customers to find her.
Citing landmarks for directions was a useful tool.
And it doesn't get much easier than "Right next door to the school."

But to improve their city's image, the council rolled new rules out.
No longer would prostitution be allowed –
Within 250 yards of a schoolhouse.
The more the city cloaked itself in an atmosphere of piety,
The less tolerant the townsfolk were of Ada's notoriety.
Some folks will cite society's right to legislate morality.
But is it really just insistence on some distance and locality?

That Ada would be told she had to move was easy to predict.
So it was no surprise to her when judge Shievley issued the edict.
She thought it would all blow over, so she decided to ignore it.
After all, some of her best customers were citizens who'd voted for it.
The judge didn't want to press the case,
So he granted her a sixty-day "floater"
To make the transition easier. (He wasn't trying to goad her.)
But Ada knew that her address gave her a leg up on the competition,
So she maintained her residence beyond the judge's permission.

The magistrate couldn't tolerate this affront to his authority,
So he made up his mind to give the boot to Ada's illicit sorority.
He drove his buggy to Ada's place to enforce the law's demands.
(He was a judge, so he could take the law into his own hands.)
Ada saw the judge approach, but she didn't feel contrite.
She wasn't about to move an inch without putting up a fight.
She wasn't going to bend her knee. She wasn't going to beg.
And she didn't care that the judge was there to make her shake a leg.
Some folks have strong convictions about what's allowed within their town,
But Ada was not going to take her eviction lying down.

The judge didn't know what kind of response
This stubborn madam planned on,
But he was there to make it clear she didn't have a leg to stand on.
The judge was stern and somber. This was not a social call.
But he was distracted by the fact that Ada's cast iron stove
Leaned up against the wall.
He considered it a fire hazard to have that stove in disrepair.
Just then Ada came rushing at him, swinging her stocking in the air.
He wondered if this was some new kind of exotic entertainment.
But what happened next was the criminal context
That led to Ada's arraignment.

The judge had heard that Ada's place was anything but dull,
But he didn't expect that stocking to crash down upon his skull!
He was fairly staggered by the force of the stocking's blow,
Because Ada had stuffed that missing stove leg down into its toe!
She got in a couple more good licks before the deputy subdued her.
She had the judge where she wanted him, and he was not going to elude her.
She was expressing her frustration. She was taking it out on Shievley.
And by the time she was disarmed, his blood was flowing freely.

They took Ada off to jail, and the judge's head was bandaged.
He was badly bruised and battered, but his will had not been damaged.
The wounded judge went back to court and worked for several more hours.
(Apparently he drew upon some extra-legal powers.)
For those in the docket that afternoon, it really was a pity.
From the look on his face, it was clear in their case,
That justice would not be pretty.
At the end of the day, the judge went home, and spent a few days in bed.
It took a while to recover from this attempt to stove-in his head.
Ada had always been able to use her legs to her own advantage,
But to knock some sense into that judge was more than she could manage.
In spite of all the prominent citizens that Ada's girls had bedded,
Her encounter with the law had been particularly hard-headed.

Most of us are prone to judge, but none of us is perfect.
And any of us might find ourselves on the wrong end of a verdict.
One person's predilection is another's impropriety.
And a whim of jurisdiction might ostracize you from society.

Ada engaged in a naked trade and some folks didn't approve.
But their righteous rage might have been assuaged
If she'd only been willing to move.
She had a reputation for being tough and gritty.
But social norms can be more relaxed on the outskirts of a city.

So if you're having one of those days where you wish you'd stayed in bed,
Or if vicious circumstances leave you hanging by a thread,
When the law comes knockin' it is wise to do some preppin'.
And don't wait until things get too hot to improvise a weapon.
Some folks think it's their duty to enact and enforce their prude laws.
But how many of us are comfortable with the government in our boudoirs?
Mankind's baser urges are not easily dismissed.
And remember that a silken glove can hide an iron fist.

Miracle Mike, "the (Headless) Wonder Chicken"

I first heard about this story on National Public Radio's "Wait, Wait, Don't Tell Me" when pioneer shock-rock musician Alice Cooper (Vincent Furnier) was being interviewed about having allegedly bitten the head off a live chicken during a performance. It turned out that he hadn't. Someone had apparently thrown a live chicken onto the stage and, in those pre-social media days, a legend had grown from rumor and repeated exaggerations. I was struck at the time with the irony that people had been willing to believe that Alice would do such a thing because it was perfectly in keeping with the stage persona he had cultivated, and yet by the time of the NPR interview his shock rock career had long ago morphed into one of successful entrepreneurship and public philanthropy in my home town of Phoenix, Arizona.

I was also taken with the irony that a headless chicken had lived for more than eighteen months while being fed from an eyedropper, only to die from getting a kernel of corn lodged in its throat. I wondered if this too, (and maybe the entire story) might be the product of runaway imagination, or in this case, rural legend. So I did a little research, and...it turns out that the story of Mike the headless chicken is true! One of Colorado farmer Lloyd Olsen's roosters survived being beheaded in 1942 and toured the country as a macabre avian celebrity. Articles were written about him in both <u>Time</u> and <u>Life Magazines</u>. Today he has his own web and Wikipedia pages, featuring pictures! It was the picture of farmer Lloyd holding the decapitated head (which was also taken on tour) that colored my perception of the situation. The facts that "Mike" came from a farm in Colorado (in which a few years of my early boyhood were spent) and died in Arizona (my natal state), placed his tragic tale squarely within the geography of my focus on the events of western history. And as for meeting the requirements of my attraction to quirkiness, as the saying goes, Hollywood couldn't have written a better script.

I may perhaps have treated the Olsens somewhat unfairly in my version of these events. (My speculation about their contemplation of insurance fraud is admittedly heavy handed.) I am now writing from a time in which animal rights are much more a part of the fabric of our society than they were in the 1940's, and every good story needs a villain. Given the economy of the times, I can't say that I wouldn't have followed the same course as did the Olsens had I been in their position, but revisionist interpretations of social mores provide a convenient platform on which to raise philosophical and ethical questions. I also don't know for a fact that the Olsens ever actually stated that Mike was like a member of their family. Such statements are not uncommon regarding our pets, but given that the "pet" in question was a headless chicken, it would be a little weird to have made such a claim. Between these things and the dark humor inherent in the documented events, there was no way I could ignore such a story once it had been brought to my attention.

Also in keeping with my M.O., I have freely exaggerated regarding events, motives, and probably even some of the cities mentioned as being stops on Mike's national tour. But apart from these few caveats, the rest of this stuff actually happened! So which came first – life imitating art, or art imitating life?

Miracle Mike, "the (Headless) Wonder Chicken"

It was just another ordinary day, out there on the Olsen's farm.
And the visit of farmer Lloyd's mother-in-law
Wasn't seen as a cause for alarm.
She'd come to visit her daughter before, so Lloyd knew just what to expect.
His wife would fry up a chicken, and her mother was fond of the neck.
His wife's chicken breasts had won many contests,
And her legs were the best in the land,
But how one could savor a chicken neck's flavor
Was more than Lloyd could understand.
But he shouldered his axe, because he had the knack
For rating the cocks, hens and chicklings.
His wife was a wizard with drumsticks and gizzards,
And his taste buds were already tickling.

But the choice of which chicken to take back to the kitchen
Was more than mere gastronomy.
Because Lloyd's feathered crop ranked right up near the top
At generating his farm's economy.
Now an egg-laying hen is a farmer's best friend,
So naturally they weren't considered.
And a passel of pullets would not fill their gullets
Whether fried, fricasseed, or frittered.
So a rooster seemed the logical choice for a date with the chopping block.
And farmer Lloyd had several of those among his avian stock.
And the best candidate for the dinner plate would be easy to detect.
Lloyd wouldn't need a booster to see which rooster held its head most erect.
And as he held his chosen victim down
With its neck stretched across the wood,
He swung the axe in deference to his mother-in-law's preference
To leave as much neck as he could.
The farmer reflected he'd probably beheaded a thousand chickens by now.
And he was relaxed as he brought down the axe with an E-I-E-I-Ow!
Off came the head and that chicken bled,
But it didn't stop flapping its wings.
Lloyd thought he'd been hexed because what happened next
Was a strange and unnatural thing.

Now you might think that after one's head is removed,
The enthusiasm for life would be dampened.
But that rooster didn't go running around
Like a bird to which that had just happened.
It just wandered away leaving Lloyd in a daze
And wondering what he'd just witnessed.
But he couldn't reject his growing respect for that rooster's physical fitness.
The next morning Lloyd went out to the yard
To search for the corpse of that chicken.
He thought he should hasten to find its location
Lest the vultures its bones would be pickin'.
But a scan of the skies showed nary a sign of a carrion bird or a buzzard.
And this lack of a swarm seemed so outside the norm
That it left Lloyd a little bit flustered.
But he hadn't expected to feel so unprotected
From the shock of his next discovery.
That headless bird seemed unperturbed
And had made an astounding recovery!
It scratched at the ground and pecked around
As if searching for grain or for bread.
And under its wing which it held like a sling –
It carried its own severed head!

Well, you couldn't blame Lloyd for feeling annoyed.
His nerves had just taken a lickin'.
His senses were blasted – he was flabbergasted
By the sight of that zombie chicken!
This lack of closure cost Lloyd his composure,
And it took time to recover his nerves.
But after a while he just had to smile at the lengths Life will go to preserve.
And where some might have run to fetch a shotgun
To finish off such a monstrosity,
He saw that, though cluckless, this bird wasn't luckless.
It was surely a scientific curiosity.

So he loaded him up in his old pickup truck
And drove over the Utah state line.
He knew for a certainty that at the university
He'd find fine agricultural minds.

Some biological antiquarians and startled veterinarians
Examined and then they explained him:
Lloyd was so circumspect at preserving the neck,
He'd left a great deal of the brainstem.
And a fortunate clot at just the right spot
Had stopped the hemorrhage and bleeding.
And the blood that had thickened had rescued this chicken.
Now good care was all he was needing.
The rooster's reactions were nervous contractions,
Not matters of executive function.
Despite his endeavors, Lloyd's axe had not severed
The spine at a critical junction.
It wasn't a miracle. The case was empirical.
A demonstration of the life force most primal.
'Though he'd have no precision at making decisions,
It was clear that this bird had no rival.
They were not ambivalent; there was no equivalent.
This rooster was clearly unique.
And with thanks to Lloyd, they were overjoyed
He'd allowed them a scientific peek.
Their imaginations were fired; academic papers were inspired.
They'd really never seen the like.
A bird of such fame was in need of a name,
So Lloyd christened him "Miracle Mike."

Now Lloyd had never been one to crow,
But Mike's reputation was starting to grow.
So rather than squander his chance or shirk it,
He booked his bird on the carnival circuit.
At grand openings and fire sale clearances,
Mike's schedule was crowded with public appearances.
County fairs and freak show hollers. Lloyd insured that bird for $10,000!
At circuses, in side show tents, the public paid their twenty-five cents.
They bought the right to gawk and stare,
And talk about Mike like he wasn't even there.
They said he strutted like a politician, down at the legislature.
"But how can he eat when he's got no beak?
He's some kind of freak of nature!"
Some said he was the devil's spawn. Some said it was preposterous.

Meanwhile Mike was maintained with water and grain
From an eyedropper down his esophagus.

They didn't know how long Mike's fame would endure,
So they booked him on a national tour.
And that's when the plot began to thicken
For "Miracle Mike, the Wonder Chicken."
Cleveland, Pittsburgh, Denver, Tucson…
The Olsens egged their golden goose on.
New York to San Diego with hardly a rest.
They relied on Mike to feather their nest.
The tour went on for a year and a half.
They lived high on the hog off their fatted calf.
And as the word of this bird got spread around,
The media heralded Mike's renown.
From Atlantic City to Newport News, Lloyd was giving interviews.
And the reporters wrote down what he said:
"He's a robust specimen of a chicken, except for not having a head."
At the top of his neck, it was more like a deck –
A fact that he shouldered irreparably.
'Though he wore no crowns, he grew to eight pounds.
(His head was displayed separately.)
He'd refused to heed life's ultimate curfew,
And a poet had lauded his avian virtue:
"A fowl that hates so much to die, there must be some good reason why."
Was it something special in his genes?
He was featured in Time and Life Magazines.
Many fans congratulated this chicken decapitated,
But the rumors that fame had gone to his head seemed greatly exaggerated.

In those days few had set their sights on the establishment of animal rights,
So few would criticize the Olsen's dealings.
And just because they saw fit to display their chicken for profit,
That didn't make them callous or unfeeling.
This headless barnyard oddity was their legitimate commodity,
And he had more than met this chief requirement.
They saw no contradiction in cashing in on their chicken.
They socked away a nest egg for retirement.

Then one night in Arizona, in a room in a cheap motel,
Mike got the midnight munchies, but it didn't go so well.
He was feeling a trifle peckish, and maybe a bit forlorn.
And when another rooster crowed at the break of dawn,
The Olsens' gravy train was gone – Mike had choked on a kernel of corn.

The Olsens had always liked to say that they thought of Mike
As if he was a member of their family.
And they claimed that exploitation played no part in their relations.
Still Mike's death was none-the-less quite a calamity.
When the Olsens saw Mike's corpse they were filled with remorse
And they wept, and they wailed, and they cried.
They were shocked and dismayed. There'd be no insurance paid
If this was seen as a case of suicide.
But if they could devise that Mike's demise
Had been caused by a fox on the prowl,
Their insurance would be covered when they claimed what they'd discovered
Was really a case of murder…most fowl.
But fabricated proofs wouldn't cover up the truth
About what had made their prize rooster die:
Mike's own midnight snacking was what had sent him packing
To that Great Eternal Barnyard in the sky.
And under duress they'd have little success of pinning Mike's death on a fox.
And they knew to their shame that they were to blame
For leaving Mike's cage door unlocked.

But was his death really an accident? Or was he a victim of greed?
Maybe he felt detached because the Olsens made the scratch
While he worked for chicken feed?
Was it existential dread that drove him from his bed
And interrupted his slumbers?
(He couldn't get back to sleep by counting sheep,
'Cause he didn't have a head for numbers.)

And if we read between the lines, there's cause for consternation.
Could Mike have rebelled against being compelled,
And attacked his lack of self-determination?
Could he have grown tired of never being inspired
And simply performing by rote?

Was his lack of free will the bitterest pill that finally stuck in his throat?
His life had been a spectacle for the mob, and a puzzle for the professors.
But the joke would be on them if he had finally cast off
The yoke of his oppressors.
There's little respect for a chicken's intellect,
Which some have described as feeble.
And it's hard to wrap one's head around concepts that are so cerebral.
As we ponder the perversities of this case, the surface we've barely scratched.
But in the end it's slim pickin's if you've counted your chickens
Before they've actually hatched.

So if you are a barnyard star, try to keep your ego in check.
You may want to fledge, but living on the edge
Can sure be a pain in the neck.
Best to rule your own roost and not be seduced
By the lure of fortune and fame.
There's a lot to be said for just keeping your head.
There's a high price for playing this game.
So don't ruffle your feathers, lest the stress and the pressures
Prevent you from feeling relaxed.
Better to be called a chicken who's alive and who's kickin'
Than to see all your hopes get the axe.

But maybe you've got a plan to take command
And to see your aspirations take wing.
Better keep your head down, don't go strutting around.
Castigation is bound to sting.
And while it might be thrilling to make the kind of killing
That allows you to get the heck out,
Your head on a plate may be the only reward
For being willing to stick your neck out.

Epilogue:
Some experts like to champion the cause of Homo sapiens
As the apex of the Almighty's creations.
And they note that lesser creatures are not equipped with features
To enable them to rise above their stations.
And according to this plan, God meant the hand of man
To tame the wild and cultivate dominion.

And the higher up, the gladder, here on evolution's ladder.
But maybe that's a matter of opinion.
And maybe, in all fairness, the burden of awareness
Is something we'd be happier not bearing;
To be free of vexing notions, and emotional explosions,
And just go through the motions without caring.
The price of human gain has been worry, stress and strain
And it has taken us from the sublime to the obscene.
But for all that we've attained with our mighty mammalian brains,
We can't survive an encounter with a guillotine.
I remember I once read that the poet Emily Dickenson said
That "Hope is the thing with feathers."
And certainly hope's the thing that makes us fashion wings
And helps us soar above constraints and tethers.
But in ordinary lives, hope is lucky to survive
The crushing disappointments that one weathers.
And it teases with the lie that despite today's dark sky,
Tomorrow holds the key to all Life's treasures.
When the randomness of chance and fickle circumstance
Entangles us and with our dreams conspires,
Hope helps us escape from the frying pan
But we burn in the fire of our desires.

The Scales of Justice

The gist of this story comes from an anecdote told by Fletcher Fairchild in <u>Those Early Days, Old Timers' Memoirs of Oak Creek, Sedona, and the Verde Valley Region of Northern Arizona</u>. The details of the story as related in my poem are true up to the point where you encounter the word "creel". From there on, my poem is mostly a fabrication. Fairchild's anecdote provides no details as to what may have actually happened to the fish, although he does attest to their measurements. He mentions that, while Heckethorn was well thought of in the community, he and his uncle later heard that Heckethorn had shown the fish around and claimed to have caught them himself. And so he concludes, "You see, there was larceny in those days too." Fairchild and Rodin's attempt to organize a search party and Heckethorn's involvement with a church feast and his subsequent remarks are elements of my own creation.

The Scales of Justice

Every fisherman tells two kinds of tales —
Those of triumph and those of dismay.
There's the epic struggle that landed the prize.
There's the one that got away.
And whether these are guys who tie their own flies,
Or just use the worms that they dig,
You can bet you are going to be hearing these words,
"I swear that that fish was THIS BIG!"
But a fisherman's boasts fall on skeptical ears
If the fish isn't there to convince.
And a fish out of water's a transient thing;
Doesn't keep well as hard evidence.

Back in Sedona's halcyon days, Oak Creek was well known for its trout.
And Bill Rodin of Flagstaff spotted one in a pool
That he knew was worth bragging about.
He determined the best way to catch such a fish
Was to cast his line in at night.
By the light of a fire he'd make that fish tire, and finally give up the fight.
So by the light of the stars he returned to that hole,

In the company of his nephew, Fletcher.
They climbed over boulders
And through tough bear grass,
With Rodin acting as thresher.
They built a big fire
And cast out their bait,

Then sat back while nothing much happened.
Fletch had never heard of fishing at night,
And he passed in and out of cat nappin'.
He awoke to find that their lines were still slack.
Silently he questioned Bill's sanity.
He doubted the existence of the great, wily fish —
Just a fiction of his uncle's own vanity.

Suddenly something hit Rodin's line hard, and Fletcher's line also went taut.
And for several minutes fish and fishermen sparred
As a creekside battle was fought.
Fletch landed a prime specimen of speckled brown trout,
About fourteen inches in length.
But Rodin was engaged in a furious bout.
His fish showed considerable strength.
Man and fish pitted wits for ten minutes or more
In a test of each other's endurance.
Then Bill finally brought that great fish to the shore,
While Fletch held the net as insurance.
Bill proved a consummate fisherman that night,
And his prize was a trophy to be treasured.
He'd pulled a great lunker from its underwater bunker.
Twenty-six inches it measured!

Then Bill and his nephew returned to their camp,
And they slept the sleep of the victorious.
They awoke refreshed with the dewy dawn,
Having dreamt sporting dreams that were glorious.
The fish were salted and wrapped in ferns
To preserve them for their homeward journey.
But Bill and Fletcher weren't eager to return.
They wanted to continue their tourney.
They ran into old man Heckethorn, a well-respected neighbor.
He said that he'd soon be heading for home,
And he'd deliver those fish as a favor.

A few days later Bill and Fletcher returned.
(Their clothes were now smelling quite rankly!)
But when they asked Rodin's wife what she thought of their fish,
She only looked at them blankly.
"I'm sure I don't know what you're talking about.
The only fish that I've seen,
Are those trout in the creels that you're holding right now,
Which I hope you have already cleaned."
Bill and Fletcher exchanged covert glances.
Their nerves were now slightly on edge.
Surely something bad must have happened,

To keep that old man from his pledge.
Their pulses now started to quicken.
Their fears were just starting to whelp.
Maybe somewhere poor Heckethorn lay stricken,
In desperate need of their help!
They dashed down the streets of Flagstaff
To gather more men for their search.
That old man was highly regarded. They couldn't leave him in the lurch!
But as they ran past an open church doorway,
They heard loud voices raised in a toast.
And praises were spoken of Heckethorn, who stood in the midst of the host.
And as Bill and Fletch gave a listen, they recognized the voice of the priest,
Who rose to commend "Brother Heckethorn"
For providing those fish for their feast!
"If you'd mounted those fish as trophies," he said,
"They would have been a feast for the eyes.
But you chose instead to share them with us, in spite of their prodigious size.
You're a man of rare generosity, who rises above worldly things.
Such delicious fish to provide for our dish,
Surely earned you your angels wings!"

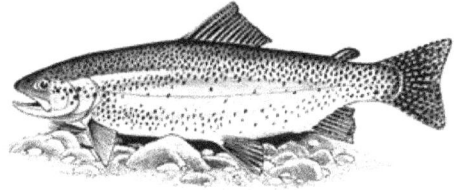

Then old man Heckethorn cleared his throat,
And began to address the crowd.
In his voice they detected a satisfied note.
They could tell he was feeling quite proud.
"My friends, I am deeply honored," he said, "to receive such a commendation.
For I have to admit that while fighting those fish,
I faced moments of great trepidation.
That Leviathan fought like no fish ever has,
And it pushed me to my very brink.
As if Satan himself had stationed it there, as a test of my faith I should think!
It was clear from the first pull that it gave on my line,
That fish was no ordinary trout.
And I needed my wits and a firmness of mind
Lest it drown me in spiritual doubt!
But the good Lord put man upon this green Earth
To exercise dominion over nature.
And that infernal fish was a challenge to me
To express my opinion of danger.

And it was the thought of you, my loyal friends,
That gave me strength and determination.
And in that lonely hour I drew on that power
To triumph in the name of salvation.
There are times when a man must look into his soul,
And conquer his personal demons.
And as I yanked that fish from its watery hole,
I could swear I heard Lucifer screamin'!
So I thought it was the least that I could do,
To give you a taste of my conquest.
And may it be a source of strength unto you,
When engaged in a similar contest.
I'm really just a humble man, seeking harmony with my neighbors.
We all must do the best that we can, and appreciate each other's labors."

Then came congratulations and laughter,
And those men all shouted "hoo-ray!"
And in the face of this moral dilemma, Bill and Fletcher just ambled away.

Now a fisherman's luck is a matter of chance, and so is a quest for glory.
And a fisherman's fame can be greatly enhanced
If he's willing to alter his story.
And who's to dispute that that fish isn't his, or to accuse him of mendacity,
When the trophy that dangles on the end of his line
Testifies to his story's veracity?
It's easy to succumb to the siren's song of a larcenous opportunity,
Or to suppress one's sense of right and wrong
If one thinks that one has immunity.
One can use deception to give the impression
He's a big fish in his own local pond,
But admiration and praise will soon fade away
If his word's not as good as his bond.
But as the poets say, the truth will out,
And it's hard to conceal from one's neighbors.
And accomplishment's glow can be shadowed by doubt
When attained by another man's labors.

Yet sometimes the fish avoids the hook, and still makes off with the bait.
And sometimes the truth gets overlooked, no matter how long we may wait.

So may those big fish always rise to your bait.
May they grant you your fisherman's wish.
And may the laurels you claim never have to be weighed
On the scales of another man's fish.
Heroes may prove to have feet of clay.
Resolution can be firm or squishy.
So have a code for those things that you do and you say,
Lest your story be judged to be fishy.

Waggin' the Dragon's Tale

This story was printed in the *Tombstone Epitaph* on April 28, 1890. It was claimed that these stalwart dragon slayers even brought back a small sample, cut from a corner of the monster's wing, and that a subsequent expedition was planned to further examine the remains and validate the discovery. If any such expedition ever ventured out, it does not seem to have been reported. (After all, it was only a flying dragon, not gold.) And the area's latter nineteenth century inhabitants may not have been the most scientifically motivated of peoples. In its This Date in Arizona History column, the *Arizona Republic* (the modern descendant of the *Arizona Republican*, founded May 19, 1890) mentioned that on October 7, 1926, three 4 inch thick, 12 inch wide, and 14 inch long teeth were found in a dry lakebed near Quitobaquito, in southern Arizona. "The find recalled an old Papago legend of a monster said to have lived in the lake." This legend, or another similar tale, may have been the aegis for the journalistic fancy that appeared in the *Epitaph*. The article's verbiage does not reflect modern political sensibilities, since it uses the now-discarded term "Papago" rather than the tribally-preferred Tohono O'odham ("Desert People"). "Papago" is a Spanish derivation of a derogatory term used by some Piman groups who competed with the O'odham for resources. It is loosely translated as "bean eaters".

John Myers Myers, writing in <u>Legends and Tales of the Old West</u> (1962), cites a story by an earlier Western writer named Horace Bell, who told of a winged dragon that lived in the foul-smelling waters of California's Lake Elizabeth (formerly Laguna del Diablo) and was allegedly seen by multiple witnesses. According to this account, some hunters took several shots at it which apparently caused it to fly away to the east where Myers speculates that it may have been the same dragon of the *Epitaph* story (which he says appeared on its pages in 1884). If this is actually the case, its flight from southern California may account for the Tombstone cowboys' observation that it seemed to be tired, and the discrepancy in the dates might indicate that the *Epitaph* re-ran some of its stories, perhaps to fill space on slow news days.

Richard Kimball, writing in *Territorial News* in November, 2015, goes into greater detail about the Lake Elizabeth creature, drawing on descriptions starting around 1830 when a Spaniard named Don Pedro Carrillo first reporting seeing it. According to Kimball, Carrillo's observations were later collaborated by American settlers in the 1850s, who claimed to have heard "unnatural screams in the night, as well as strange noises coming from the lake." Still later, Don Chico Lopez and Don Chico Vasquez were forced to abandon their ranch by the lake due to the monster's depredations. Finally a Basque named Miguel Leonis came into possession of the land along the lakeshore and, like others before him, found that when he shot at the creature, his bullets seemed to bounce off its skin. In frustration, Leonis is alleged to have struck its face with the butt of his rifle, causing it to retreat into the lake and then, a few days later, re-emerge and fly away to the east. This alleged dragon is described as having "huge bat-like wings, a neck as long as a giraffe, the head of a bulldog, [and] six legs." It was claimed to be "at least fifty feet long, [and] in addition...had a nauseating smell."

Kimball's article includes pictures that were alleged to have been taken of both the Lake Elizabeth dragon, and of the creature described in the *Epitaph* article. These pictures are obvious fabrications (Kimball doesn't claim that they are legitimate) and in neither case do the creatures shown match the descriptions given of the alleged dragons. He also cites an article attributed to the *Sacramento Daily Record-Union* of March, 1882 describing another flying monster of varying descriptions "looking something like a crocodile" and having six two-foot long wings and three pairs of feet.

At a place called Crack-in-the-Rock, on the Wupatki National Monument in northern Arizona, I have seen a petroglyph that seems to depict a winged dragon in flight. The Crack-in-the-Rock area has hundreds of ancestral Puebloan petroglyphs presumed to date back to the first half of the previous millennium (circa 1000 – 1500 CE), and even though this dragon-like image was carved in the area, it may have been the work of a Chinese laborer of the latter 1800s who hiked several miles north from where the Atlantic and Pacific Railroad was laying its ties and, in the spirit of American tourists who carved their names and the dates of their visits, added something emblematic of his own culture. In the late 1980s, an FBI sting operation arrested two brothers from the Springerville area in connection with illegally excavating and selling prehistoric artifacts from various northern Arizona sites. One of the brothers told investigators that he sold a pottery fragment to a wealthy Chinese collector on which was painted what appeared to be a dragon in flight. This piece of the puzzle is now gone, so its veracity cannot be ascertained. It is possible that ancient pottery designs might have resembled such a creature. And certainly those giant teeth found at Quitobaquito didn't just materialize out of nothing.

As far as the story that appeared in the *Epitaph* goes, the motives of seeking fame and notoriety implied in my poem are complete speculation on my part. It is very possible if not probable that the two cowboys who claimed to have done the killing were entirely fictitious and that the entire story was concocted by the *Epitaph's* editor or one of its contributors. (See The Gunfight at Big Hat, Joseph Mulhatton, and Gladwell Richardson and the Burden of Reputation.) And if the alleged cowboys really did exist, I'm willing to bet that whatever they encountered was seen through a lens of 100 proof whiskey.

Similar types of stories in other Arizona papers of the time involved claims of the discovery of the remains of an ancient ship "several miles from the Fort Yuma Road" (*The Weekly Arizonian*, December 17, 1870) and of fossilized whale bones many miles east from the Colorado River. It was speculated that the alleged whale must have swam from the Sea of Cortez, up the Colorado and thence some miles inland along the Gila River, presumably during a flood stage.

Waggin' the Dragon's Tale

Strange tales have been told by those who rode Arizona's rugged trails.
And sometimes a fact ain't exactly exact when you scrutinize details.
Deceptions, lies, and alibis can often be expedient.
And it turns out a fact can expand or contract
If it makes it more convenient.

A cowboy's job keeps him away from the mob as he toils in anonymity.
If attention is desired, what might be required is imagination and creativity.
Two ranchers returned from a mysterious sojourn
Out between the Huachucas and the Whetstones.
And they told a story sure to bring them glory,
And to make sure their names would get known.
They'd heard their share of cowboys declarin'
And engaging in campfire braggin'.
But those stories would pale compared to their tale
Of finding and killing a dragon!

They'd been riding along through the desert,
When they came upon a great winged beast.
They said it looked like a giant alligator,
With a mouth full of razor-sharp teeth!
It could only fly a short distance,
So they judged it must be rather tired.
And any resistance was futile
When they took up their Winchesters
And fired.
They boldly gave chase to the monster,
'Though their horses were quite terrified.
They just kept pumping lead into its hideous head,
Until it rolled over and died.

And then they carefully measured it. They wanted to leave no doubt.
The head alone was longer than a man –
Eight feet from its neck to its snout!
The body was ninety-two feet long, the belly was five feet wide!
And they measured it twice, so they knew they weren't wrong,
And no one could say that they lied.

The eyes were the size of dinner plates,
The wings spanned a hundred-sixty feet!
This lizard was truly gigantic – its shadow would darken a street!
This horrible gargantuan reptile had soared across southwestern skies.
Yet remarkably no one else had seen it…

Well were they ever in for a surprise!
The tale of them killing this dragon
Would surely earn them a reputation.
So they galloped their horses for Tombstone,
To bask in some public adulation.
They told their tale to the editor
Of the *Tombstone Epitaph*,
And he agreed to publish the story,

But fate would have the last laugh.
He used all the details they mentioned, and listed every one of their claims,
But advertising demanded column inches, so he ended up omitting their names.

Incredible claims from sun baked brains have helped to sell newspapers.
And readers delight when editors write about outlandish capers.
An outrageous story sounds better when one's under the influence of whiskey.
And when told in the heat of the moment, wild windys might not seem so risky.
But hallucinated "facts" are hard to redact when one is stone cold sober.
And loose-tongued allegations can cause remorse and frustration
When you wake up with tomorrow's hangover.
If your name is attached to the schemes that you've hatched,
It can cause you some embarrassment.
But if your name gets in print for what you did while bent,
Then you might be in line for some harassment.
If your claims aren't constrained by the rules of the game
That most folks define as normality,
Then a loose-lipped fable's likely to get you labeled
As a resident of an alternate reality.

So if you're not shy about tellin' lies,
And exaggeration doesn't make you quaver,
When credibility's in doubt, if your name gets left out,
Someone might just have done you a favor.

These Boots Were Made For Dyin'

Growing up in Phoenix, I heard lots of snake lore. As a guide in Arizona's outback, I've heard much of the more phobic examples repeated by otherwise well-educated and urbane adults. Some of the more far-fetched examples include the belief that a snake can take its tail in its mouth in order to form a hoop and roll itself in pursuit of hapless humans, or that a snake cut into sections can re-join itself and continue to live as if the partitioning had never happened. This last we may owe to the "Join or Die" flag created by Benjamin Franklin in 1754. On August 25th, 1893, *The Arizona Republican* reported that a party from Mesa, camping at Willow Springs in the Superstition Mountains, claimed to have killed a rattlesnake 79 feet long with 97 rattles. The Superstitions are a very aptly-named mountain range. As a young man I camped in its canyons many times. In my experience, the kinds of creatures one encounters there are often contingent on what one may have been ingesting.

A dozen different varieties of rattlesnakes can be found within Arizona's borders. It is reported that the most commonly-spoken words immediately preceding a rattlesnake bite are, "Hold my beer and watch this."

The Arizona Republic reports that on August 24th, 1929, a Willcox ranch woman used a shovel and a hoe to kill 13 rattlesnakes in her yard. This one is not only true, but also not that uncommon. In 2013, a statue titled, "The Not-So-Gentle Tamer" by sculptor Debbie Gessner was unveiled in Prescott Valley. The statue portrays a woman dressed in her pioneer best – she's even wearing gloves – holding a shovel in one hand and a decapitated rattlesnake in the other. The rattler's disembodied head lies near the toe of her boot. From these things we may draw two corollaries: Arizona pioneer women were tough and determined; and, in Arizona, rattlesnakes are considered garden variety pests.

My poem is inspired by a popular and often-repeated story from my boyhood years, concerning an unfortunate Arizona widow who was said to have lost three husbands before the still potent rattlesnake fangs were found embedded in her first husband's boots. This of course would not be possible, but nonetheless made for a great campfire tale (especially if one could surreptitiously shake something to simulate the maraca-like sound of the snake's rattles at the climactic moment).

JOIN, or DIE.

These Boots Were Made For Dyin'

The woman raised her tear-filled eyes and cried, "Oh Lord, why me?"
As she knelt beside the freshly-filled grave of husband number three.
They had just embarked on their honeymoon,
A week at a western dude ranch.
They'd barely caught their breath when his sudden death
Put an end to their second-hand romance.
And as if this loss of wedded bliss would not serve to depress her,
It was found there was venom in his veins – just like his predecessor!
Her first husband died in the countryside.
He'd succumbed to a rattlesnake bite.
But now rumor suggested that the poison was ingested,
And the coroner hadn't gotten it right.
And while they might accept that the first husband's death
From a rattlesnake's bite was true,
This third death raised suspicion because the coroner and mortician
Said the same thing about husband number two!
The neighbors called her grief a sham. They called her a "black widow".
She'd done in husbands one and two; now number three was ditto.
They claimed she had a secret vial of potent rattler venom,
And she'd devised some devious means to get that venom in 'em.
There were calls to arraign her on a murder charge.
The editorials were delirious.
Three dead spouses in such rapid succession
Was more than a little mysterious.

But the mystery was solved when the law got involved,
And the widow regained her good graces.
A detective discovered the sinister thread that snaked through all three cases.
He examined the boots the first husband had worn
On the day that the rattlesnake bit him.
They'd been given in turn to the next two men
Because in each case those fine boots had fit him.
But the bride hadn't lied nor had she connived to cause their hearts to calcify.
She wasn't in cahoots with those love-cursed boots.
They were in fact her alibi.

The wife's penchant for thrift in bestowing this gift
Helped him put two and two together.
He discovered the rattlesnake's fangs broken off,
And still sticking through the cowboy boot leather!

This wasn't haunted homicide, supernaturally depraved.
No jealous husband striking back for revenge from beyond the grave.
No one was embroiled in an evil love's coils; these deaths were almost habitual.
Love's hopes had been punctured at the fatal juncture
Of their ankles and venom residual.
That rattlesnake's fangs had caused their death pangs
Even though they'd been snapped off in Tucson.
Each new man had been scratched and fatally dispatched.
And they'd literally died with their boots on.

When you walk down the aisle,
You're wearing a smile.
You're joyful and light-hearted.
And you'd never suppose
You could be killed by the clothes
That were worn
By the dearly departed.
You exchange your vows,
Say your "thees and thous",
And you may think
That you've paid all your dues.
But to avoid unseen shocks,
Wear some extra thick socks
If you walk in another man's shoes.

Animal Magnetism

C. L. Sonnichsen relates the apocryphal story on which my poem is based in the introduction to <u>Billy King's Tombstone</u>, in which he also describes various forms of insect, arachnid, reptile, and avian combats which were popular among the town's inhabitants.

Tombstone and Bisbee got their starts in the latter 1870's. Both grew rapidly to large populations composed of miners and the various categories of purveyors who catered to their needs – merchants, ranchers and farmers, restauranteurs, blacksmiths, gamblers, preachers, prostitutes, laundries, liveries, opium dens, and those who speculated in land or capital (a practice known as "grubstaking").

The foundation of Bisbee's economy was copper. Its famous Copper Queen mine produced ores that assayed at 23% copper, with silver and gold as byproducts. Copper ores are generally considered profitable at 3 or 4%. The initial claim that would be developed into the Copper Queen and surrounding Warren Mining District was valued at forty million dollars. George Warren, for whom the mining district is named, was a character of questionable integrity who gambled away his one-ninth interest in the Copper Queen on a drunken bet that he could outrun a man riding a horse. A picture of him posed with a pick and shovel provided the model for the image of a miner used on one of the versions of Arizona's Official State Seal.

Tombstone's wealth was obtained from silver ores that assayed as high as $2,000 a ton. Prospector Ed Schieffelin, who staked the initial claims, had been told that all he would find in the surrounding Apache-infested hills was his own tombstone. During its decade-long "boom" period, $38 million of mineral wealth was extracted, its population grew from about 1,000 to 7,000 persons, and it has been claimed that two out of every three of its buildings were saloons or gambling halls. Of approximately 480 deaths recorded during this same period, only 43 were alleged to have occurred from natural causes, the majority of the others being attributed to gunshot wounds, morphine and alcohol overdoses, heart disease, mine explosions, and being run over by trains.

Lawlessness and violence were so pervasive in the Tombstone – Bisbee region of Cochise County that on May 3, 1882 President Chester A. Arthur threatened to place the whole of Arizona Territory under martial law. Acting Governor John Jay Gosper vented his frustration with the southern citizens in the Territorial press: "The people of Tombstone and Cochise County in their mad career after money, have grossly neglected local self-government until the lazy and lawless element of society have undertaken to prey upon the more industrial and honorable classes for their subsistence and gains." George W. Parsons, a member of Tombstone's Committee of Vigilance recorded in his diary during March of 1880, "I was never in a place or business before where there was so much chenanniging [sic] carried on."

In a sense it might be said that the Bisbee – Tombstone rivalry ended in a draw. Both were forced to rebuild after fires gutted their business districts. Underground water flooded Tombstone's mines in the 1890s and brought its boom years to an end. The giant Phelps-Dodge and other mining corporations continued to extract some ores until 1950. Phelps-Dodge also finally acquired all of the mining interests around the Bisbee area and continued operations there until the 1970s. Both communities evolved later economies based on tourism.

"Sas-per-ella" is the phonetic pronunciation for a beverage that is actually spelled *sarsaparilla*. The beverage was originally brewed from the roots of a plant which is a member of the lily family (genus *Smilax*). It was originally used for medicinal purposes, but has now become more of a carbonated soda drink somewhat akin to root beer.

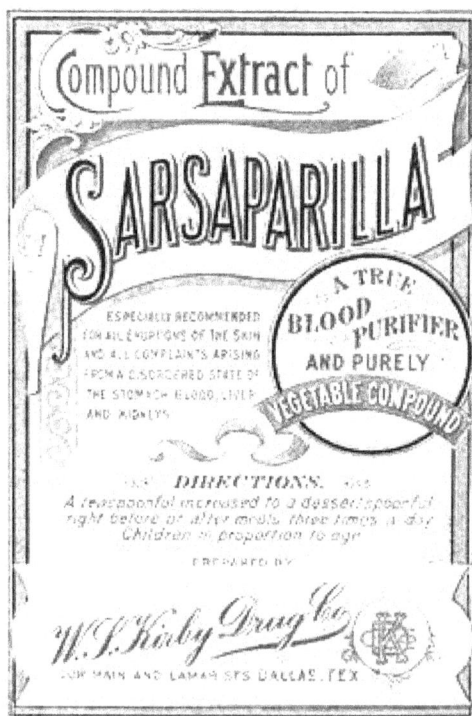

Animal Magnetism

The noise in the Tombstone saloon that night
Showed the men were in high spirits.
They stood three deep crowded 'round the bar. All straining to get near it.
For someone new to work his way through he'd need a crowbar or a spatula.
They were throwing down bets on a fight to the death
Between a centipede and a tarantula.
And odds were laid and money was paid for some to jabber and gawk
As a Gila monster tangled with the talons of a hawk.
And it was safe to assume that in the bar's back room
Feathers flew in a furious cock fight.
All the shouting and betting and wagered blood-letting
Was getting these men to feel all right.
New schemes were conceived and some suckers deceived
Amid curses and jokes and fables,
When a man from a rival town burst in, and strode among the tables.
And some jumped up and stood on chairs to keep their feet out of reach,
Because a snarling, hissing bobcat strained at the end of the stranger's leash!

The wildcat growled and scratched and prowled,
Lapping liquor from overturned glasses.
And the boys were distraught as they desperately thought
About how they might save their asses!
They could tell that cat's master might threaten disaster.
He was tall. He was dark. He was muscular.
Protest or objection might mean vivisection.
It was clear he was one tough customer.
And he seemed almost bored as he spat on the floor.
Then his face filled with contempt.
"You boys don't scare anyone anymore. You're dirty and unkempt.
I've just come down from Bisbee," he said, as his lip curled in a sneer.
"And I pity the man who tries to stand between me and a beer.
Us Bisbee men live for blood and sin in a town where copper is Queen.
Down in this rats nest you're just second best.
You don't amount to a hill of beans.

You like to pretend you Tombstone men are dangerous and rough.
But I'm here to tell you face to face, you're just not tough enough!
This snarling bobcat on my leash that makes you fuss and fret,
To me is just a kitten. I keep him as a pet.
One look at my cat and half of you spat out
Your drinks and revealed that you're yella.
You'd be more at ease gently sippin' some tea or the foam from a sas-par-ella!
So just sit on your hands, all you dapper Dans.
When I'm gone all your women will miss me.
By the time you get home, you'll be there all alone
'Cause they've moved up to join me in Bisbee."

And those that remained all backed away and stood there in shuffling silence.
And they were ashamed that their spirits were tamed
And restrained in a state of compliance.
But one Tombstone man didn't even turn around. He did not seem perturbed.
He didn't show the slightest frown or sign he was disturbed.
If the stranger's words annoyed him, he did nothing to make him aware of it.
Because he had a little friend he knew would soon take care of it.
He didn't unchain a grizzly bear, he didn't unleash a lion.
He didn't use a scorpion to show his will of iron.
He reached into his pocket and removed a scaly companion,
And tossed it at the stranger's feet with nonchalant abandon.

The stranger gasped in horror, and he seemed about to swoon.
He gave a shriek of terror and ran out of the saloon.
That man and his cat were both gone just like that!
How much happier then had the room grown.
And the boys were amused at the speed of his shoes
Making tracks as he fled out of Tombstone.
His bluff had been called and his plans had been stalled
In spite of his manly virility.
But they had to admit that his get-up-and-git
Had been done with amazing agility!
Then the Tombstone men gave attention again to their whiskey as before,
While their friend retrieved his pet rattlesnake from off the barroom floor.

There are lots of things in modern life of which to be afraid:
Traffic jams, e-mail scams, politicians on a crusade;
Shopping mall mobs, down-sized jobs, or a notice from the I.R.S.;
Warranty expirations, even holiday celebrations, when taken to excess.
Inflationary losses, crabby bosses, and rising unemployment.
Like albatrosses we bear the crosses that lessen our enjoyment.
But if you're trying to make a point about whose is the tougher town,
It's better sometimes to bare your fangs than to pussy-foot around.

Prohibition

Arizona was the tenth state to adopt Prohibition. Twenty-five states had outlawed the production, sale, and distribution of alcoholic beverages (aside from homemade wine made from fruit) prior to the passing of the 18th Amendment to the Constitution which made it a federal requirement. The national law took effect on January 16, 1920, and within a week, small portable stills were for sale all across America. Whiskey could still be obtained by getting a doctor to proscribe it, and it is reported that doctors made about $40,000,000 on the sale of these prescriptions between 1921 and 1930. In what seems ironic from our present-day perspective, one of the staunchest supporters of Prohibition was the Ku Klux Klan. However after the Klan fell into disgrace in 1925 its advocacy was seen as a disparagement to Prohibition enforcement.

Arizona's adventure with Prohibition was rich in episodes ranging from the comical to the hypocritical to the tragic. Of the four cases mentioned (with embellishments) in my poem, one is apocryphal and the other three are documented. There are no records of fish being flavored by liquor dumped into rivers or absorbed by worms, and the story of the moonshiner accidentally striking it rich due to the explosion of his still may have only been wishful thinking. Several stills were discovered in Jerome's mineshafts. U.S. Marshals found two in the same shaft in 1919. Jerome Deputy Sheriff Fred Hawkins discovered a still hidden in the rafters above a 1,000 foot long tunnel dug to bring water to fields from the Verde River. The moonshiners had to wade through water four feet deep in the tunnel to reach their still.

Other documented examples include a 1926 raid on a dairy farm by Yuma County sheriff's deputies who found more moonshine than milk. The haul included 200 gallons of liquor and 750 gallons of mash. In 1928 the Navajo County sheriff raided the Holbrook City Hall and confiscated 65 gallons of bootleg whiskey in 13 kegs that were hidden under the floor boards. And in Jerome, liquor was obtained for the Annual Volunteer Firemen's Ball by having a police officer – who was also a member of the Fire Department – make enough raids to confiscate the necessary 20 or so gallons. Jerome deputies also participated in the discovery of the largest still ever found by Arizona Revenue agents. It had a 450 gallon capacity! Of course quality is just as important as quantity, as was recorded in a 1929 court case wherein a Mesa police constable testified that the moonshine produced in his town was far superior to that produced in that of the neighboring town of Gilbert.

Of course the unregulated production of strong alcoholic spirits is dangerous. Government laboratory tests on one-hundred samples of bootleg liquor seized by federal officers in Arizona in 1923 showed that all were poisonous. Arizona led the nation in Prohibition enforcement effectiveness that year, with an estimated 97% conviction rate. In April of 1925, a still located in downtown Cottonwood exploded in the middle of the night. The resultant fire lasted three days and burned down most of the town's commercial district.

Citizens crouched under wet mattresses to allow them to get close enough to fight the flames with the few small hoses that were available.

During the years of Prohibition deaths from alcohol poisoning and cirrhosis of the liver sustained higher rates and those suffering from alcoholism and the victims of domestic violence related to alcohol addiction had almost nowhere to turn for help. Violent crime increased as armed gangs organized to control the production and distribution of liquor within rivaling territories, and it has been estimated that illegal sales of bootleg liquor across the nation generated about six billion dollars in untaxed revenue.

Prohibition

Arizona's Territorial reputation was scorned and sneered at nationally.
But its citizens desired acceptance. They wanted statehood passionately.
And when at last that status was granted, they thought they'd show contrition.
They countered public opinion, and adopted Prohibition.
But the citizens didn't give a damn about the legislature's thinking.
It would take more than a government ban to make them give up drinking.
And thus it was that the Temperance Creed became the government's mission.
But resistance would be guaranteed in response to Prohibition.

In an abandoned shaft near old Jerome a moonshiner hid his still.
He was glad the miners had excavated so deep into that hill.
It kept his work from the prying eyes of Revenue agent predators,
And kept his still's whereabouts unknown to unscrupulous competitors.
The locals liked his liquor, and they made frequent buys,
So he often had to go to town to get some more supplies.
And 'though he did not like to have to leave his hooch unguarded,
He hid his juice behind the sluice when off to town he started.
One day while he was at this task, away from his abode,
A burner that he'd left aflame caused his still to explode!
This loss of income could have led to curses, tears and whining.
But they say that even the darkest cloud can have a silver lining.
The virtues of honest labor are frequently extolled.
He returned to find his exploded still had exposed a vein of gold!
And thus we see how dreams of wealth can awaken to fruition
When accident and enterprise collide with prohibition.

For those tea-totaling Revenue men one problem that awaited
Was what to do with all the booze that they had confiscated.
To burn it meant controlling flames, and of course they risked explosion.
So to dump it in a river was a method often chosen.
They dumped a thousand gallons in the Rio Salado in 1923.
And it made the local river folk as happy as could be.
While they might have liked to take a drink, they none-the-less were tickled
To find that all the fish they caught had already been pickled!

The Sheriff poured out liquor on the Pima County courthouse lawn.
And that brought out the fishermen from all around Tucson.
They didn't mind that the grass was damp as they hunted for nightcrawlers.
The bait they prized had been baptized with hooch worth $20,000.
They never complained if their pants got stained
As they gathered up worms quite briskly.
They slithered in a brine of contraband wine and potent bootleg whiskey.
And the fish they hooked and later cooked filled them with much delight.
That absorbed rot gut gave the fish they caught an extra tangy bite.
It's long been said that alcohol goes hand in hand with fishin'.
Those inebriated fish were an unexpected wish that was granted by Prohibition.

Some agents dumped their captured stuff down the plumbing of a Phoenix hotel.
But the employees got wise and tapped those pipes, and syphoned it off to sell.
Some say that a new door opens whenever an old door closes.
The cops were unaware of what was going on right under their very own noses.
With the police supplying the product, those entrepreneurs did quite well.
They engaged in unsavory recycling in the bowels of that hotel.
From the time that they started to peddle their brand,
To the time they were made to confess,
They could scarcely keep up with the public's demand.
You could say they were flushed with success.
The bootleggers maintained a constant supply despite what the cops confiscated.
And those lawmen couldn't quite figure out why their efforts seemed so constipated.
The law proscribed booze should not be imbibed,
And it was up to the cops to enforce.
No matter how much they dumped, they still remained stumped,
Because they couldn't locate the source!
They couldn't abide the public's appetite for intoxicating swill,
And it was their job to see that the mob would bow to the government's will.
But humans are frail and the threat of jail couldn't make them rise above it.
So the lawmen's target was to dry up the market and get to the bottom of it.
Their Commander was growing impatient. It was an intolerable situation.
And he issued orders that landed like mortars, exploding with his frustration.
The government looked weak if it couldn't curtail the public's illicit enjoyment.
So cut the crap and shut off their tap, or look for some other employment!

The hotel employees kept selling that squeeze while the cops were being skunked.
And their customers could literally be described as getting stinking drunk.

But after some sleuthing and nosing around, the cops finally picked up the scent.
And the trail inevitably led them down to that hotel's bootlegging basement.
They caught the hotel staff red-handed, and they confiscated the liquor.
But they still got reprimanded. Those criminals had been slicker.

This wasn't a very complex case. It didn't have many facets.
But they'd unwittingly aided those criminals by liquidating their assets.
Unintended consequences of decisions can prove to be mind-numbing.
And doubtless their Commander's derision was bound to be forthcoming.
Their expeditious use of the plumbing had resulted in criminal gain.
And now they feared that their careers were circling the drain.
They'd done their best and they'd made the arrest, but the evidence was in disarray.
They'd thwarted public craving, but any chances of saving
Their jobs had all been pissed away.
The irony here is ample – both the tragic and the comic.
And this episode's surely an example of trickle-down economics.
And thus the straight and narrow path can still lead to perdition.
For the criminal knows that profit flows through the code of Prohibition.

In 1933, the government gave up, and Prohibition was repealed.
And consumption came out into the open, from where it had been concealed.
The Revenue men could smile again, and they laid aside their axes.
The government knew that by legalizing brew they'd at least collect some taxes.
Draconian public policies will always divide a society.
It leaves a bad taste when someone undertakes to mandate our sobriety.
A Nanny State may try to dictate that spirits should not be available,
But it's often been found that the moral high ground
May be dry, but it's not unassailable.

Life is full of stresses, and people will seek relief.
It can come to blows when you try to impose on personal belief.
You may claim a moral imperative in an attempt to garner votes.
But no one will swallow that narrative if you're ramming it down their throats.
An unwise law always sticks in the craw. It only breeds sedition.
It doesn't stifle appetite, or weaken one's volition.
This seems an obvious lesson, but it took 19 years to learn it.
Government's business is safety and protection. Lifestyle choices don't concern it.

Alcohol abuse is evil, and many have cause to hate it.

But in the end alcohol is less lethal if we allow, but regulate it.

People are going to quench their thirst. They won't wait for permission.

And if you don't condone, they'll just make their own.

That's the lesson of Prohibition.

The Legend of Ol' Brind,
or How Brin's Mesa Got Its Name (Redux 2015)

I made significant revisions to this earlier work, which was originally published in <u>The Facts Keep Gettin' in the Way of the Story</u> in 2013, so I've included the up-dated text here. In the revisions, I corrected my erroneous interchanging of the words bull and steer, and added a little more to the context of what galled the cowboys about their inability to capture "Old Brind" or "Ol' Brin" as he was also known. The original long-horned cattle that grazed the ranges of the Mogollon Rim's red rock country had the reputation of being truly wild. Some of the area's pioneers reported cattle that had evaded capture for ten or twelve years! It was said that such cattle learned to recognize the sound of shod horses and would hide behind boulders or even lay down to conceal themselves behind fallen logs. If one was able to get one's rope around the neck of such an animal it would often be necessary to tie it to a stout tree for two or three days until thirst made it docile enough to be led in.

The Legend of Ol' Brind (Redux 2015)
(How Brin's Mesa Got Its Name)

Come listen my children, and I'll tell you how
Two cowboys murdered a noble cow.
It was back in those days when you worked to survive,
And hardly a cowhand is still alive
Who remembers that bull with the brindled hide,
Whose freedom was a thorn in every cowboy's side.
Old Brind was a Texan of the long-horned kind.
He'd gone wild for so long he would not be confined.
And all the Verde cowboys longed for the glory they'd win,
If they'd be the one to finally bring him in.
Each new season of freedom only added to his stature.
For more than five years now he'd evaded their capture.
The ranchers and wranglers were feeling downhearted.
At every encounter Brin left them out-smarted.
Many had tried him, and to their chagrin,
That bull was triumphant again and again.
His independence confounded them. It gnawed at their pride.
Ol' Brin' was so confident, he didn't even try to hide.
He ranged on that mesa southeast of Dry Creek.
Tough country for cowpokes, no place for the meek.

But one morning Ed Dickinson and Jimmy Van Deren
Spotted Ol' Brind at the edge of a clearing.
And feeling their oats, they lit out with abandon.
And darn all the luck if their ropes didn't land on!
But before they could pull that wise bull to the ground,
He'd spotted a thicket, and headed them down.
Now, Jimmy and Ed knew that those trees would sure kill them,
But they didn't much cotton to the shame that would fill them
If they lost their ropes and their friends should get wind of it,
They reckoned they never would hear the end of it.
For a cowboy who loses his rope is a greenhorn tenderfoot
Subject to everyone's scorn.

A cowboy tries to balance pride in work and reputation.
But this bovine had exceeded their allowance for frustration.

Jim and Ed were sick and tired of the way Old Brind outfoxed them.
And they swore to be revenged
On this longhorn who had mocked them.
They couldn't face the shame of losing this game
If they were unable to pen him in.
And if he got away, could they ever say
That they felt like real full-grown men again?
They would not allow him to make them look like fools.
So they gave themselves permission to play outside the rules.

So pulling their guns, they shot Old Brindle down.
Then they coiled up their ropes and rode back into town.
Confessing their deed would have brought them dishonor,
So they never let on that Ol' Brind was a goner.
Cow punchin' with their friends, can't you just imagine the tension?
Jim and Ed "shot the bull" whenever Brind's name got mentioned.
They kept it a secret, a memory hushed.
But when the carcass was discovered, they were seen to blush.
And finally the truth all came out in the wash.
And Jimmy and Ed were both kidded and joshed.
Those cow-killin' cowboys never captured Ol' Brin'.
And neither of them's got a mesa named after him.

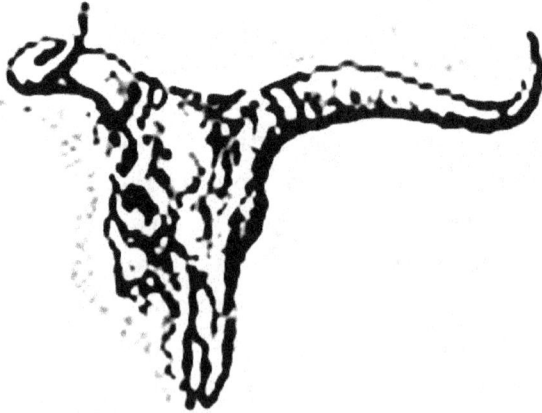

About the Author

Native Arizonan Michael Peach has an abiding love for the prehistory, history, and topography of the American southwest. He also loves satire and making people laugh. He graduated *cum laud* from Northern Arizona University and earned a Master's degree in theatre from California Institute of the Arts. He is a Certified Trainer of Interpretive Guides with the National Association for Interpretation, a former presenter for the Arizona Commission on the Humanities, and has been performing his original living history programs at the Sedona Heritage Museum and various venues throughout Arizona since the late twentieth century.